Selected Poems

Frank O'Hara

Selected Poems

Edited by Mark Ford

ALFRED A. KNOPF   *New York*   2008

THIS IS A BORZOI BOOK
PUBLISHED BY ALFRED A. KNOPF

Copyright © 2008 by Maureen Granville-Smith
Introduction copyright © 2008 by Alfred A. Knopf, a division of Random House, Inc.

Grateful acknowledgment is made to the following for permission to reprint previously published material:
City Lights Books: "Adieu to Norman, Bon Jour to Joan and Jean-Paul," "Ave Maria," "Cornkind," "The Day
Lady Died," "Fantasy," "For the Chinese New Year & For Bill Berkson," "A Little Travel Diary," "Music,"
"Naptha," "On Rachmaninoff's Birthday (Quick! A last poem before I go)," "Personal Poem," "Poem en Forme
de Saw," "Poem (I watched an armory combing its bronze bricks)," "Poem (Instant coffee with slightly sour
cream)," "Poem (Khrushchev is coming on the right day!)," "Poem (Lana Turner has collapsed!)," "Rhapsody,"
"Song (Is it dirty)," "St. Paul and All That," "A Step Away from Them," and "Steps" from *Lunch Poems* by Frank
O'Hara, copyright © 1964 by Frank O'Hara; "[And leaving in a great smoky fury]," "Epigram for Joe,"
"[The fondest dream of]," "Fou-rire," "[It is 1:55 in Cambridge, pale and spring cool]," "Kein Traum,"
"[On the vast highway]," "A Party Full of Friends," "Song (I'm going to New York!)," and "To Dick" from
Poems Retrieved by Frank O'Hara, copyright © 1996 by Maureen O'Hara, Administratrix of the Estate of
Frank O'Hara. Reprinted by permission of City Lights Books.
Grove/Atlantic, Inc.: "Aus einem April," "Blocks," "Chez Jane," "For Grace, after a Party," "The Hunter,"
"Les Étiquette jaunes," "Mayakovsky," "Meditations in an Emergency," "On Seeing Larry Rivers' *Washington
Crossing the Delaware* at the Museum of Modern Art," "Poem (At night Chinamen jump)," "Poem (The eager note
on my door said 'Call me')," "Poem (There I could never be a boy,)" "Radio," "River," "Sleeping on the Wing,"
"A Terrestrial Cuckoo," "The Three Penny Opera," "To the Film Industry in Crisis," and "To the
Harbormaster" from *Meditations in an Emergency* by Frank O'Hara, copyright © 1957 by Frank O'Hara.
Reprinted by permission of Grove/Atlantic, Inc.

The poems in this collection were originally published in the following works:
The Collected Poems of Frank O'Hara, copyright © 1971 by Maureen Granville-Smith,
Administratrix of the Estate of Frank O'Hara (Alfred A. Knopf);
Early Writings, copyright © 1977 by Maureen Granville-Smith (Grey Fox Press);
Lunch Poems, copyright © 1964 by Frank O'Hara (City Lights Books);
Meditations in an Emergency, copyright © 1957 by Frank O'Hara (Grove Press);
Poems Retrieved, copyright © 1977 by Maureen Granville-Smith (Grey Fox Press);
Selected Plays, copyright © 1978 by Maureen Granville-Smith.

Library of Congress Cataloging-in-Publication Data
O'Hara, Frank, 1926–1966.
[Poems. Selections]
Selected Poems / by Frank O'Hara ; edited by Mark Ford. — 1st ed.
p. cm.
ISBN 978-0-307-26815-0
I. Ford, Mark, 1962– II. Title.
PS3529.H28A6 2008
811'.54—dc22
2007042865

Manufactured in the United States of America
First Edition

Contents

Appendix: Prose

Introduction

"I love your poems in *Poetry*," James Schuyler wrote to Frank O'Hara after reading a batch that included "Radio" and "On Seeing Larry Rivers's *Washington Crossing the Delaware* at the Museum of Modern Art" in the March 1956 issue of the Chicago magazine. "In that cutting garden of salmon pink gladioli," he continued, "they're as fresh as a Norway spruce. Your passion always makes me feel like a cloud the wind detaches (at last) from a mountain so I can finally go sailing over all those valleys with their crazy farms and towns. I always start bouncing up and down in my chair when I read a poem of yours like 'Radio,' where you seem to say, 'I know you won't think this is much of a subject for a poem but I just can't help it: I feel like this,' so that in the end you seem to be the only one who knows what the subject for a poem *is*."

Schuyler's elaborate metaphors, and his account of the way the poems have him physically "bouncing up and down" in his chair, suggest much about the unique and liberating nature of Frank O'Hara's poetry. Unlike the tasteful, carefully crafted "salmon pink gladioli" on offer elsewhere in the magazine, O'Hara's poems enable Schuyler to break free "(at last)" from the sterile security of terra firma and embark on a panoramic survey of life in all its surreal variety. But the sense of the sublime the poems make possible is achieved not by addressing themselves to particular subjects but by a passionate, unembarrassed responsiveness to whatever happens to happen, however incongruous or seemingly trivial. Like so many of O'Hara's readers, Schuyler finds himself galvanized by an injection of "immortal energy," to borrow a phrase from "Radio"—even though the poem's ostensible subject matter (Saturday-afternoon classical-radio schedules) may seem none too promising. What matters, and gets communicated, is the poet's self-reliant assertion: "I just can't help it: I feel like this."

O'Hara disliked and distrusted theories of poetry but was in no way naive about his own procedures, which result, in his best work, in a style of writing that somehow manages to fuse immediacy and excitement with a glamorous hyper-sophistication and extreme self-consciousness. "I'd have," he tells us in "My Heart,"

> the immediacy of a bad movie,
> not just a sleeper, but also the big,
> overproduced first-run kind. I want to be
> at least as alive as the vulgar.

When asked by Donald Allen for a statement to accompany his selection in the ground-breaking anthology *The New American Poetry* of 1960, O'Hara responded with a spoof manifesto entitled "Personism," in which he playfully ridiculed the very notion of writing according to some program or set of preconceived ideas: "You just go on your nerve. If someone's chasing you down the street with a knife you just run, you don't turn around and shout, 'Give it up! I was a track star for Mineola Prep.' " As for poetic form and other technical aspects of poetry, "that's just common sense: if you're going to buy a pair of pants you want them to be tight enough so everyone will want to go to bed with you." His own personal breakthrough occurred, we learn, shortly after lunch with Leroi Jones on August 27, 1959, "a day in which I was in love with someone (not Roi, by the way, a blond). I went back to work and wrote a poem for this person. While I was writing it I was realizing that if I wanted to I could use the telephone instead of writing the poem, and so Personism was born."

While O'Hara's poems do often seem to unfurl with the randomness and intimacy of a telephone call (and how he would have adored cell phones!), they are also unobtrusively guarded, as he puts it in "Biotherm (for Bill Berkson)," "from mess and measure." From the outset of his career, O'Hara knew he wanted to develop a kind of poetry radically different from that being written and published by most English-language poets. In a talk given in 1952 at the Club—an artists' forum on East Eighth Street where painters, and occasionally poets, exchanged ideas and insults—O'Hara targeted especially those laboring under the "deadening and obscuring and precious effect" of T. S. Eliot. "And after all, only Whitman and Crane and Williams, of the American poets," "Personism" declares, "are better than the movies." Early O'Hara reveals the influence of Williams, certainly, but also O'Hara's immersion in numerous European (mainly French) poets and, in particular, the work of Rimbaud, Mallarmé, Lautréamont, Apollinaire ("I dress in oil cloth and read music / by Guillaume Apollinaire's clay candelabra"), René Char, André Breton, Pierre Reverdy, Mayakovsky, Pasternak, Rilke, and Lorca.

O'Hara was born in Baltimore in 1926, and grew up in Grafton, Massachusetts. His parents were both of Irish descent, and he attended Catholic schools. Initially, he intended a career in music, as a pianist or reviewer or composer. He was enrolled for a time in the New England Conservatory, but his studies there were interrupted by

America's entry into World War II. O'Hara enlisted in late 1944 and served as a sonar-man on the destroyer U.S.S. *Nicholas* in the South Pacific, and in operations off Japan itself. On his demobilization in 1946, he applied to Harvard and was accepted, again to study music; but after a freshman year of increasing disappointment with the music department, he switched his major to English and devoted himself to the writing of poems that he submitted to the scrutiny of his close friend Edward Gorey and the poet-on-campus, John Ciardi. A number were accepted for publication in *The Harvard Advocate*, one of whose editors was John Ashbery. The two met, however, only shortly before Ashbery graduated in the summer of 1949 and moved down to New York.

While it is true that the poems O'Hara wrote as an undergraduate, and then as a master's student in creative writing at Ann Arbor in Michigan, are occasionally, as Ashbery has suggested, "marred by a certain nervous preciosity," they also reveal a poet deliberately experimenting with all manner of unfamiliar and iconoclastic idioms, in search of a distinctive and effective style of his own. The most successful seem to me those—like "Autobiographia Literaria," with which this selection opens, or "A Pleasant Thought from Whitehead" or "The Critic"—that deploy a faux-naif tone to celebrate O'Hara's triumphant sense of his own poethood:

> And here I am, the
> center of all beauty!
> writing these poems!
> Imagine!

In the extraordinary "Memorial Day 1950," he offers a more extended and combative vision of his metamorphosis into a poet, one "tough and quick" enough to think with his "bare hands and even with blood all over / them." It's in this poem also that O'Hara begins the copious acknowledgment of inspirers and artistic heroes so characteristic of his work: It was Pablo Picasso who made him tough and quick (with a little help from "the world"), and further tributes are paid to Gertrude Stein, Max Ernst, Paul Klee, the Fathers of Dada, Auden, Rimbaud, Pasternak, and Apollinaire.

But O'Hara's poems are full not only of the familiar names of the illustrious but of those of his numerous friends. (Of course, some of these, such as Willem de Kooning, were already famous, and others, like Larry Rivers or Jasper Johns, would become so.) One of O'Hara's earliest attempts to make poetry out of his social life was "A Party Full of Friends," first published in *Poems Retrieved*. It mentions many of those who crop up most often in O'Hara's poems—Violet (V.R. or Bunny Lang), Jane (Freilicher), Hal (Fondren), Larry (Rivers), John (Ashbery), and so on. The sassy exuberance of his early experiments in surrealism is here applied to commemorating a party that Ashbery hosted in his furnished room on West Twelfth Street while O'Hara was staying with him during a Christmas break from Ann Arbor in 1950. The poem initiates what one might call O'Hara's mythopoeic gossip mode:

Violet leaped to the piano
stool and knees drawn up
under her chin commenced to
spin faster and faster sing-
ing "I'm a little Dutch boy
Dutch boy Dutch boy" until
the rain very nearly fell
through the roof!

Not since Alexander Pope has a poet so filled his work with the names and doings of his contemporaries, though while Pope expended his genius on presenting his enemies as dunces, O'Hara set about celebrating the exchange of inspiration and innovation, of art and love and rumor, among the painters, poets, novelists, dancers, filmmakers, composers, and musicians who made up his ever expanding circle and his first readership. "You are really," he wrote to Kenneth Koch in "Poem (The fluorescent tubing burns like a bobby-soxer's ankles)"

the backbone of a tremendous poetry nervous system
which keeps sending messages along the wireless luxuriance
of distraught and hysterical desires so to keep things humming

O'Hara had a similarly catalytic effect on his artist friends, and liked to keep things "humming" at a steady pitch of excitement. One of his most famous poems, "Why I Am Not a Painter," wittily explores the mysteries of the relationship between poetry and painting, in particular his and the painter Mike Goldberg's shared fascination with the possibilities of abstraction. "It was too much," Goldberg remarks of the SARDINES he has removed from his painting, while O'Hara's long poem about orange never actually gets around to mentioning the color:

There should be
so much more, not of orange, of
words, of how terrible orange is
and life. Days go by. It is even in
prose, I am a real poet. My poem
is finished and I haven't mentioned
orange yet. It's twelve poems, I call
it ORANGES. And one day in a gallery
I see Mike's painting, called SARDINES.

O'Hara engaged in a series of intriguing collaborations with painters such as Larry Rivers, Norman Bluhm, Jasper Johns, and Joe Brainard, and as a reviewer for *ARTNews* and as a curator at the Museum of Modern Art did much to promote the work of the artists who meant most to him. "His presence and poetry," Koch recalled in an essay of 1964, "made things go on around him which could not have happened in the same way if he had not been there." Certainly the concluding lines of "A Party Full of Friends" suggest he realized on this early visit to New York that he had found there his ideal milieu:

> Someone's going
> to stay until the cows
> come home. Or my name isn't
> Frank O'Hara

The Manhattan of O'Hara's poetry is a quasi-mythic city alive with nuance and possibility. "515 Madison Avenue / door to heaven?" ask the opening lines of "Rhapsody." At times the city assumes a distinct personality, as in "To the Mountains in New York," where it is figured as a brash, aging vamp, "noisy and getting fat and smudged / lids hood the sharp hard black eyes," but more often it serves as the site and inspirer of O'Hara's restless, fractured, shimmering fantasies, or as radiant backdrop to his intense friendships and brief or prolonged love affairs. In "Homosexuality," which is explicitly about cruising, he tallies up the merits of various latrines—"14th Street is drunken and credulous, / 53rd tries to tremble but is too at rest"—before poignantly voicing the secret thought of all who come to the city in quest of the good life: " 'It's a summer day, / and I want to be wanted more than anything else in the world.' "

The poems that won most plaudits in O'Hara's tragically shortened lifetime were those he called his "I do this I do that" poems, such as "A Step Away from Them," "The Day Lady Died," "Adieu to Norman, Bon Jour to Joan and Jean-Paul," all set in the present tense of O'Hara's lunch hour: "It's my lunch hour . . . ," "It is 12:20 in New York a Friday . . . ," "It is 12:10 in New York and I am wondering . . ." These were collected in his immensely popular City Lights collection of 1964, *Lunch Poems*, for which O'Hara himself composed the jacket copy:

Often this poet, strolling through the noisy splintered glare of a Manhattan noon, has paused at a sample Olivetti to type up thirty or forty lines of ruminations, or pondering more deeply has withdrawn to a darkened ware- or firehouse to limn his computed misunderstandings of the eternal questions of life, co-existence and depth, while never forgetting to eat Lunch his favorite meal . . .

In fact, he normally typed up his midday ruminations upon return to his office in the Museum of Modern Art after his cheeseburger and glass of papaya juice, but the image here presented of a poet capable of writing any time, any place, was essentially a true one. James Schuyler, who shared an apartment with O'Hara in the mid-fifties, recalled one morning when he and Joe LeSueur began to tease O'Hara about his ability to compose at speed and on demand, at which "Frank gave us a look—both hot and cold—got up, went into his bedroom and wrote 'Sleeping on the Wing,' a beauty, in a matter of minutes." "Is there speed enough?" this poem appropriately demands, a question that reverberates throughout O'Hara's oeuvre.

Yet despite his frequent public displays of poetic facility, even close friends were surprised at the extraordinary bulk of his *Collected Poems* when it appeared in 1971; I once weighed it on my kitchen scales and found it came in at just over three and a half pounds. And that was not all; in the years following its success (it won the National Book Award and demolished once and for all the notion that O'Hara was some kind of poetic dilettante or lightweight), Donald Allen discovered enough unpublished material to fill two further volumes, *Early Writing* (1977) and *Poems Retrieved* (1977). In 1978 Full Court Press published his *Selected Plays*. O'Hara's drama is, I think, worthy of more attention and performance than it has received, and I have included here the second version of *Try! Try!* This short verse play is at once a brilliant comedy of bad manners; a highly original take on that old chestnut, the love triangle; and a devastatingly witty exploration of the way O'Hara felt his war experiences had shaped his sense of modernity. The veteran Jack returns home, his "feet covered with mold," only to find his wife, Violet, in the arms of the snake in the grass John. In a vivid and moving speech, Jack recounts how his initial martial exhilaration curdles into self-doubt and despair; when he is eventually shot by a sniper on a beach in the Pacific, he feels almost relieved: "I fell like a / sail, relaxed, with no surprise. / And here I am." But if he expected the story of his sufferings to move or shame his auditors, he is soon disabused: "Do you think everything can stay the same," John demands, "like a photograph?"

No, O'Hara's work insists and illustrates, time and again. Indeed, his approach might be described as the opposite of photographic. His poetry delights in mobility, in metamorphosis, in excess, in consumption—particularly of coffee, cigarettes, and alcohol—, in interactions of all kinds, with taxi drivers, with paintings, poems, and symphonies, with friends and lovers (who else could have titled a poem "You Are Gorgeous and I'm Coming"?), with a louse he names Louise and describes trekking across his own body, with the city itself ("How funny you are today New York / like Ginger Rogers in *Swingtime*"), and of course, with the haloed stars of the silver screen whom he addresses in poems such as "To the Film Industry in Crisis," "Thinking of James Dean," and the delightful "Poem (Lana Turner has collapsed!)" that he dashed off on the Staten Island Ferry on the way to a poetry reading at Wagner College in February 1962.

> Lana Turner has collapsed!
> I was trotting along and suddenly
> it started raining and snowing
> and you said it was hailing

but hailing hits you on the head
hard so it was really snowing and
raining and I was in such a hurry
to meet you but the traffic
was acting exactly like the sky
and suddenly I see a headline
LANA TURNER HAS COLLAPSED!
there is no snow in Hollywood
there is no rain in California
I have been to lots of parties
and acted perfectly disgraceful
but I never actually collapsed
oh Lana Turner we love you get up

The state of hurry in which O'Hara presents himself here is far from unusual; in poem after poem we see him "reeling around New York," "wanting to be everything to everybody everywhere," rushing "to get to the Cedar to meet Grace," or "entraining" with Jap (Jasper Johns) and Vincent (his lover, the dancer Vincent Warren) for a weekend in Southampton at "excitement-prone Kenneth Koch's." "If I had my way," he once responded when asked if he was ready for bed after an all-night party, "I'd go on and on and on and on and never go to sleep." His last surviving poem, an elegy for the Spanish poet Antonio Machado, celebrates "purple excess" and the "soul's expansion / in the night."

O'Hara was only forty when he died as the result of injuries sustained in an accident that occurred in the early hours of July 24, 1966, after an evening spent at the home of Morris Golde on Water Island and at the discotheque in Fire Island Pines. The beach taxi in which he and his friend J. J. Mitchell were traveling broke down. As they waited for a replacement to arrive, a Jeep approaching from the opposite direction swerved to avoid the stranded taxi and travelers, and it struck O'Hara. He was taken by police launch and ambulance to Bayview General Hospital on Long Island. Despite an operation to stabilize his condition that afternoon, O'Hara died the following evening. He was buried in Green River Cemetery in Springs, where, some eight years earlier, he had visited the grave of one of his greatest heroes, Jackson Pollock. A line from "In Memory of My Feelings" is inscribed on his headstone: "Grace to be born and live as variously as possible."

A Note on the Texts

With the exception of the play *Try! Try!* the texts used in this selection were established by Donald Allen for his various editions of the work of Frank O'Hara. Allen worked with O'Hara on the compilation of *Lunch Poems* in the early sixties, and his textual decisions reflect his understanding of O'Hara's poetic ideals and compositional practices. *Try! Try!* was first published in *Artists' Theatre* (1960), edited by Herbert Machiz.

Selected Poems

AUTOBIOGRAPHIA LITERARIA

When I was a child
I played by myself in a
corner of the schoolyard
all alone.

I hated dolls and I
hated games, animals were
not friendly and birds
flew away.

If anyone was looking
for me I hid behind a
tree and cried out "I am
an orphan."

And here I am, the
center of all beauty!
writing these poems!
Imagine!

1949 or *1950*

POEM

At night Chinamen jump
on Asia with a thump

while in our willful way
we, in secret, play

affectionate games and bruise
our knees like China's shoes.

The birds push apples through
grass the moon turns blue,

these apples roll beneath
our buttocks like a heath

full of Chinese thrushes
flushed from China's bushes.

As we love at night
birds sing out of sight,

Chinese rhythms beat
through us in our heat,

the apples and the birds
move us like soft words,

we couple in the grace
of that mysterious race.

1950

4

POEM

The eager note on my door said "Call me,
call when you get in!" so I quickly threw
a few tangerines into my overnight bag,
straightened my eyelids and shoulders, and

headed straight for the door. It was autumn
by the time I got around the corner, oh all
unwilling to be either pertinent or bemused, but
the leaves were brighter than grass on the sidewalk!

Funny, I thought, that the lights are on this late
and the hall door open; still up at this hour, a
champion jai-alai player like himself? Oh fie!
for shame! What a host, so zealous! And he was

there in the hall, flat on a sheet of blood that
ran down the stairs. I did appreciate it. There are few
hosts who so thoroughly prepare to greet a guest
only casually invited, and that several months ago.

1950

5

TODAY

Oh! kangaroos, sequins, chocolate sodas!
You really are beautiful! Pearls,
harmonicas, jujubes, aspirins! all
the stuff they've always talked about

still makes a poem a surprise!
These things are with us every day
even on beachheads and biers. They
do have meaning. They're strong as rocks.

1950

MEMORIAL DAY 1950

Picasso made me tough and quick, and the world;
just as in a minute plane trees are knocked down
outside my window by a crew of creators.
Once he got his axe going everyone was upset
enough to fight for the last ditch and heap
of rubbish.
                Through all that surgery I thought
I had a lot to say, and named several last things
Gertrude Stein hadn't had time for; but then
the war was over, those things had survived
and even when you're scared art is no dictionary.
Max Ernst told us that.
                    How many trees and frying pans
I loved and lost! Guernica hollered look out!
but we were all busy hoping our eyes were talking
to Paul Klee. My mother and father asked me and
I told them from my tight blue pants we should
love only the stones, the sea, and heroic figures.
Wasted child! I'll club you on the shins! I
wasn't surprised when the older people entered
my cheap hotel room and broke my guitar and my can
of blue paint.
             At that time all of us began to think
with our bare hands and even with blood all over
them, we knew vertical from horizontal, we never
smeared anything except to find out how it lived.
Fathers of Dada! You carried shining erector sets
in your rough bony pockets, you were generous
and they were lovely as chewing gum or flowers!
Thank you!
           And those of us who thought poetry
was crap were throttled by Auden or Rimbaud
when, sent by some compulsive Juno, we tried
to play with collages or sprechstimme in their bed.
Poetry didn't tell me not to play with toys

but alone I could never have figured out that dolls
meant death.
                    Our responsibilities did not begin
in dreams, though they began in bed. Love is first of all
a lesson in utility. I hear the sewage singing
underneath my bright white toilet seat and know
that somewhere sometime it will reach the sea:
gulls and swordfishes will find it richer than a river.
And airplanes are perfect mobiles, independent
of the breeze; crashing in flames they show us how
to be prodigal. O Boris Pasternak, it may be silly
to call to you, so tall in the Urals, but your voice
cleans our world, clearer to us than the hospital:
you sound above the factory's ambitious gargle.
Poetry is as useful as a machine!
                              Look at my room.
Guitar strings hold up pictures. I don't need
a piano to sing, and naming things is only the intention
to make things. A locomotive is more melodious
than a cello. I dress in oil cloth and read music
by Guillaume Apollinaire's clay candelabra. Now
my father is dead and has found out you must look things
in the belly, not in the eye. If only he had listened
to the men who made us, hollering like stuck pigs!

                                              1950

TRAVEL

Sometimes I know I love you better
than all the others I kiss it's funny

but it's true and I wouldn't roll
from one to the next so fast if you

hadn't knocked them all down like
ninepins when you roared by my bed

I keep trying to race ahead and catch
you at the newest station or whistle

stop but you are flighty about
schedules and always soar away just

as leaning from my taxicab my breath
reaches for the back of your neck

1950

LES ÉTIQUETTES JAUNES

I picked up a leaf
today from the sidewalk.
This seems childish.

Leaf! you are so big!
How can you change your
color, then just fall!

As if there were no
such thing as integrity!

You are too relaxed
to answer me. I am too
frightened to insist.

Leaf! don't be neurotic
like the small chameleon.

1950

A PLEASANT THOUGHT FROM WHITEHEAD

Here I am at my desk. The
light is bright enough
to read by it is a warm
friendly day I am feeling
assertive. I slip a few
poems into the pelican's
bill and he is off! out
the window into the blue!

The editor is delighted I
hear his clamor for more
but that is nothing. Ah!
reader! you open the page
my poems stare at you you
stare back, do you not? my
poems speak on the silver
of your eyes your eyes repeat
them to your lover's this
very night. Over your naked
shoulder the improving stars
read my poems and flash
them onward to a friend.

The eyes the poems of the
world are changed! Pelican!
you will read them too!

1950

ANIMALS

Have you forgotten what we were like then
when we were still first rate
and the day came fat with an apple in its mouth

it's no use worrying about Time
but we did have a few tricks up our sleeves
and turned some sharp corners

the whole pasture looked like our meal
we didn't need speedometers
we could manage cocktails out of ice and water

I wouldn't want to be faster
or greener than now if you were with me O you
were the best of all my days

1950

I think a lot about
the Peachums: Polly
and all the rest are
free and fair. Her jewels
have price tags in case
they want to change
hands, and her pets
are carnivorous. Even
the birds.
      Whenever our
splendid hero Mackie
Messer, what an honest
man! steals or kills, there
is meaning for you! Oh
Mackie's knife has a false
handle so it can express
its meaning as well as
his. Mackie's not one to
impose his will. After all
who does own any thing?

But Polly, are you a
shadow? Is Mackie projected
to me by light through film?
If I'd been in Berlin in
1930, would I have seen you
ambling the streets like
Krazy Kat?
      Oh yes. Why,
when Mackie speaks we
only know what he means
occasionally. His sentence
is an image of the times.
You'd have seen all of us
masquerading. Chipper; but
not so well arranged. Air-
ing old poodles and pre-war

furs in narrow shoes
with rhinestone bows.
Silent, heavily perfumed.
Black around the eyes. You
wouldn't have known who
was who, though. Those
were intricate days.

1950

AN IMAGE OF LEDA

The cinema is cruel
like a miracle. We
sit in the darkened
room asking nothing
of the empty white
space but that it
remain pure. And
suddenly despite us
it blackens. Not by
the hand that holds
the pen. There is
no message. We our-
selves appear naked
on the river bank
spread-eagled while
the machine wings
nearer. We scream
chatter prance and
wash our hair! Is
it our prayer or
wish that this
occur? Oh what is
this light that
holds us fast? Our
limbs quicken even
to disgrace under
this white eye as
if there were real
pleasure in loving
a shadow and caress-
ing a disguise!

1950

POEM

If I knew exactly why the chestnut tree
seems about to flame or die, its pyramids

aquiver, would I tell you? Perhaps not.
We must keep interested in foreign stamps,

railway schedules, baseball scores, and
abnormal psychology, or all is lost. I

could tell you too much for either of us
to bear, and I suppose you might answer

in kind. It is a terrible thing to feel
like a picnicker who has forgotten his lunch.

And everything will take care of itself,
it got along without us before. But god

did it all then! And now it's our tree
going up in flames, still blossoming, as if

it had nothing better to do! Don't we have
a duty to it, as if it were a gold mine

we fell into climbing desert mountains,
or a dirty child, or a fatal abscess?

1950 or *1951*

THE CRITIC

I cannot possibly think of you
other than you are: the assassin

of my orchards. You lurk there
in the shadows, meting out

conversation like Eve's first
confusion between penises and

snakes. Oh be droll, be jolly
and be temperate! Do not

frighten me more than you
have to! I must live forever.

1951

POETRY

The only way to be quiet
is to be quick, so I scare
you clumsily, or surprise
you with a stab. A praying
mantis knows time more
intimately than I and is
more casual. Crickets use
time for accompaniment to
innocent fidgeting. A zebra
races counterclockwise.
All this I desire. To
deepen you by my quickness
and delight as if you
were logical and proven,
but still be quiet as if
I were used to you; as if
you would never leave me
and were the inexorable
product of my own time.

1951

SONG

I'm going to New York!
(what a lark! what a song!)
where the tough Rocky's eaves
hit the sea. Where th'Acro-
polis is functional, the trains
that run and shout! the books
that have trousers and sleeves!

I'm going to New York!
(quel voyage! jamais plus!)
far from Ypsilanti and Flint!
where Goodman rules the Empire
and the sunlight's eschato-
logy upon the wizard's bridges
and the galleries of print!

I'm going to New York!
(to my friends! mes semblables!)
I suppose I'll walk back West.
But for now I'm gone forever!
the city's hung with flashlights!
the Ferry's unbuttoning its vest!

1951

A RANT

"What you wanted I told you"
I said "and what you left me
I took! Don't stand around
my bedroom making things cry

any more! I'm not going to
thrash the floor or throw any
apples! To hell with the radio,
let it rot! I'm not going to be

the monster in my own bed
any more!" Well. The silence
was too easily arrived at; most
oppressive. The pictures swung

on the wall with boredom and
the plants imagined us all in
Trinidad. I was crowded with
windows. I raced to the door.

"Come back" I cried "for a minute!
You left your new shoes. And the
coffee pot's yours!" There were no
footsteps. Wow! what a relief!

1951

INTERIOR (WITH JANE)

The eagerness of objects to
be what we are afraid to do

cannot help but move us   Is
this willingness to be a motive

in us what we reject?   The
really stupid things, I mean

a can of coffee, a 35¢ ear
ring, a handful of hair, what

do these things do to us?   We
come into the room, the windows

are empty, the sun is weak
and slippery on the ice   And a

sob comes, simply because it is
coldest of the things we know

1951

Violet leaped to the piano
stool and knees drawn up
under her chin commenced to
spin faster and faster sing-
ing "I'm a little Dutch boy
Dutch boy Dutch boy" until
the rain very nearly fell
through the roof!
                              while, from
the other end of the room,
Jane, her eyeballs like the
crystal of a seer spattering
my already faunish cheeks
with motes of purest colored
good humor, advanced slowly.

"Poo!" said Hal "they are
far too elegant to be let
off the pedestal even for a
night" but Jack quickly and
rather avariciously amended
"it's *her* birthday," then
fell deliberatively silent
as
    Larry paced the floor. Oh
Larry! "Ouch" he cried (the
latter) "the business isn't
very good between Boston and
New York! when I'm not paint
ing I'm writing and when I'm
not writing I'm suffering
for my kids I'm good at all
three"
            indeed you are, I
added hastily with real ad-
miration before anyone else
could get into the poem, but

Arnie, damn him! had already
muttered "yes you are" not
understanding the fun of
idle protest.
        John yawked
onto the ottoman, having eyes
for nought but the dizzy
Violet, and George thought
Freddy was old enough to
drink. Gloria had not been
invited, although she had
brought a guest.
            What
confusion! and to think
I sat down and caused it
all! No! Lyon wanted some
one to give a birthday
party and Bubsy was born
within the fortnight the
only one everybody loves. I
don't care. Someone's going
to stay until the cows
come home. Or my name isn't
                Frank O'Hara

1951

A TERRESTRIAL CUCKOO

What a hot day it is! for
Jane and me above the scorch
of sun on jungle waters to be
paddling up and down the Essequibo
in our canoe of war-surplus gondola parts.

We enjoy it, though: the bats squeak
in our wrestling hair, parakeets
bungle lightly into gorges of blossom,
the water's full of gunk and
what you might call waterlilies if you're

silly as we. Our intuitive craft
our striped T shirts and shorts
cry out to vines that are feasting
on flies to make straight the way
of tropical art. "I'd give a lempira or two

to have it all slapped onto a
canvas" says Jane. "How like
lazy flamingos look the floating
weeds! and the infundibuliform
corolla on our right's a harmless Charybdis!

or am I seduced by its ambient
mauve?" The nose of our vessel sneezes
into a bundle of amaryllis, quite
artificially tied with ribbon.
Are there people nearby? and postcards?

We, essentially travellers, frown
and backwater. What will the savages
think if our friends turn up? with
sunglasses and cuneiform decoders!
probably. Oh Jane, is there no more frontier?

We strip off our pretty blazers
of tapa and dive like salamanders
into the vernal stream. Alas! they
have left the jungle aflame, and in
friendly chatter of Kotzebue and Salonika our

friends swiftly retreat downstream
on a flowery float. We strike through
the tongues and tigers hotly, towards
orange mountains, black taboos, dada!
and clouds. To return with absolute treasure!

our only penchant, that. And a red
billed toucan, pointing t'aurora highlands
and caravanserais of junk, cries out
"New York is everywhere like Paris!
go back when you're rich, behung with lice!"

1951

TO DICK

The Holy Ghost appears
to Wystan in Schrafft's
to me in the San Remo
wearing a yellow sweater.

Ghost couples, gathers, sweeps
and lashes and crashes like
wave on shingle! is blonde.
The sky opens. Such choirs

with their entangling moods
rush us, more subway than
opera, into an airdrome
filled with Palm trees and Eyes.

1952

COMMERCIAL VARIATIONS

I

"When you're ready to sell your diamonds
it's time to go to the Empire State Building"
and jump into the 30s like they did in 1929.
Those were desperate days too, but I'd no more
give up our silver mine, Belle, just because gold
has become the world standard look, than all
your grey hairs, beloved New York from whence
all the loathsome sirens don't call. They would like
to take you away from me wouldn't they? now that the fever's
got me and there're rumors of a Rush in California
and pine fields in Massachusetts as yet unindustrialized.
That's how they act to The American Boy
from Sodom-on-Hudson (non-resident membership
in The Museum of Modern Art) as if it weren't the best
little municipality in the U.S. with real estate
rising like a coloratura, no road sighs, and self-plumbing;
and more damned vistas of tundra than Tivoli
has dolce far niente. It's me, though, not the city—
oh my god don't let them take me away! wire The Times.

2

Last year I entertained I practically serenaded
Zinka Milanov when the Metropolitan Opera Company
(and they know a good thing) came to S-on-H, and now
I'm expected to spend the rest of my days in a north-state
greenhouse where the inhabitants don't even know
that the "Jewel Song" 's from *Carmen*. They think oy
is short for oysters. I may be tough and selfish, but
what do you expect? my favorite play is *William Tell*.
You can't tell me the city's wicked: I'm wicked.
The difference between your climate and mine is
that up north in the Aurora Borealis the blame falls like rain.
In the city's mouth if you're hit in the eye it's the sun

or a fist, no bushing around the truth, whatever that is.
I like it when the days are ducal and you worry fearlessly.
Minding the Governor your lover, and the witch your sister,
how they thought of the least common denominator and're dazzling!

     3
The sky has opened like a solarium and the artillery
of the pest has peddled into the feathery suffering
its recently published rhymes. How that lavender weeping
and beastly curses would like to claim the soldiers its own,
and turn the "tide" of the war! But they, shining,
mush back to The Trojan Horse, climb up, and ride away.

     4
Yes, the mathematicians applauded when the senator
proved that god never sent cablegrams or disappeared
except when voodoo or political expediency flourished,
it being sweet times, in Tammany in the 90s
and before one hated to seem too cocky or too ritzy.
One thought a good deal then of riding for pleasures
and in shrubbery of a casual fistfight Vesuvius smarting
and screaming creamed rubily as if to flush the heavens.
As the glassy fencing of sunrise in a fish market
cries out its Americanism and jingoes and jolts daily
over the icebergs of our historically wispy possum-drowsy
lack of antiquity, we know that art must be vulgar to say
"Never may the dame claim to be warm to the exact,
nor the suburban community amount to anything in any way
that is not a pursuit of the purple vices artsy-craftsy,
the loom in the sitting room where reading is only aloud
and illustrative of campfire meetings beside the Out Doors
where everyone feels as ill at ease as sea-food."

Often I think of your voice against the needles of dawn
when the dampness was operatic in Ann Arbor lilacs
and the gold of my flesh had yet to be regimented in freckles.
Now I must face the glass of whatever sliver's my smile,

each day more demanding me for what I have always tossed aside
like listening to *Erwartung* hanging by your thumbs;
I turn grey over night screaming feverishly scoreful, note
for note as I have always believed, for I know what I love
and know what must be trodden under foot to be vindicated
and glorified and praised: Belle of Old New York
your desperation will never open in *La Forza del Destino*
which was my father's favorite opera when he tried to jump
out a window on New Year's Eve in 1940, thirty days
before I ditched the stable boy who gave me the diamonds
I'm turning in today for a little freedom to travel.

1952

CHEZ JANE

The white chocolate jar full of petals
swills odds and ends around in a dizzying eye
of four o'clocks now and to come. The tiger,
marvellously striped and irritable; leaps
on the table and without disturbing a hair
of the flowers' breathless attention, pisses
into the pot, right down its delicate spout.
A whisper of steam goes up from that porcelain
urethra. "Saint-Saëns!" it seems to be whispering,
curling unerringly around the furry nuts
of the terrible puss, who is mentally flexing.
Ah be with me always, spirit of noisy
contemplation in the studio, the Garden
of Zoos, the eternally fixed afternoons!
There, while music scratches its scrofulous
stomach, the brute beast emerges and stands,
clear and careful, knowing always the exact peril
at this moment caressing his fangs with
a tongue given wholly to luxurious usages;
which only a moment before dropped aspirin
in this sunset of roses, and now throws a chair
in the air to aggravate the truly menacing.

1952

BLOCKS

1

Yippee! she is shooting in the harbor! he is jumping
up to the maelstrom! she is leaning over the giant's
cart of tears which like a lava cone let fall to fly
from the cross-eyed tantrum-tousled ninth grader's
splayed fist is freezing on the cement! he is throwing
up his arms in heavenly desperation, spacious Y of his
tumultuous love-nerves flailing like a poinsettia in
its own nailish storm against the glass door of the
cumulus which is withholding her from these divine
pastures she has filled with the flesh of men as stones!
O fatal eagerness!

2

O boy, their childhood was like so many oatmeal cookies.
I need you, you need me, yum, yum. Anon it became suddenly

3

like someone always losing something and never knowing what.
Always so. They were so fond of eating bread and butter and
sugar, they were slobs, the mice used to lick the floorboards
after they went to bed, rolling their light tails against
the rattling marbles of granulation. Vivo! the dextrose
those children consumed, lavished, smoked, in their knobby
candy bars. Such pimples! such hardons! such moody loves.
And thus they grew like giggling fir trees.

1952

OCTOBER

Summer is over,
that moment of blindness
in a sunny wheelbarrow
aching on sand dunes
from a big melancholy
about war headlines
and personal hatreds.

Restful boredom waits
for the winter's cold solace
and biting season of galas
to take over my nerves,
and from anger at time's
rough passage I fight
off the future, my friend.

Is there at all anywhere
in this lavender sky
beside the UN Building
where I am so little
and have dallied with love,
a fragment of the paradise
we see when signing treaties
or planning free radio stations?

If I turn down my sheets
children start screaming through
the windows. My glasses
are broken on the coffee table.
And at night a truce
with Iran or Korea seems certain
while I am beaten to death
by a thug in a back bedroom.

1952

RIVER

Whole days would go by, and later their years,
while I thought of nothing but its darkness
drifting like a bridge against the sky.
Day after day I dreamily sought its melancholy,
its searchings, its soft banks enfolded me,
and upon my lengthening neck its kiss
was murmuring like a wound. My very life
became the inhalation of its weedy ponderings
and sometimes in the sunlight my eyes,
walled in water, would glimpse the pathway
to the great sea. For it was there I was being borne.
Then for a moment my strengthening arms
would cry out upon the leafy crest of the air
like whitecaps, and lightning, swift as pain,
would go through me on its way to the forest,
and I'd sink back upon that brutal tenderness
that bore me on, that held me like a slave
in its liquid distances of eyes, and one day,
though weeping for my caresses, would abandon me,
moment of infinitely salty air! sun fluttering
like a signal! upon the open flesh of the world.

1952

WALKING TO WORK

It's going to be the sunny side
from now
      on. Get out, all of you.

This is my traffic over the night
and how
      should I range my pride

each oceanic morning like a cutter
if I
    confuse the dark world is round
round who
      in my eyes at morning saves

nothing from nobody? I'm becoming
the street.
        Who are you in love with?
me?
    Straight against the light I cross.

1952

34

TRY! TRY!

To Anne Meacham

JOHN

VIOLET

JACK

PLACE: *A studio.*

SCENE: *A room. A war has ended. The two are sitting on an old wicker sofa, listening to a phonograph record.*

JOHN:

I like songs about hat-check girls,
elevators, bunions, syphilis, all the
old sentimental things. It's not enough
to be thoughtful, is it?

VIOLET:

Aren't you acting terribly prewar?

JOHN:

My dear, I want you to work hard at
reinstating that wifely melancholy that
made you such a distinctive asset to
anyone "marching off" as they say. You
used to mourn for him like a model house.
Now the neighbors are all saying you've
gone down the drain. All I can say is
what a drain! I prefer to think you were
always a little too nice. "If anyone
cries in the world. . . .

VIOLET:

. . . it has to be me." Please stop trying
to cheer me up. Jesus. You're as relaxing
as a pin. I was a sweet, eager, pretty, and
energetic girl. As he remembers me, so
shall he find me. What ever made me take you
on as an added complication! You fill the

35

house. Or maybe it's me. I do burn a little
cork every time the smell of apple blossoms
drifts in the window. I haven't been burning
any lately though.

JOHN:
I could move out. I could just move out.

VIOLET:
Oh no. I want you here for evidence that I've
gone bad. I think you'll do the trick. Do
you hear a radio in the distance?

JOHN:
Don't change the subject. Why don't you wash
a few clothes before he gets back? I think
cerise would be a nice color for eventide.
Shall we mop the skylight?

VIOLET:
What's the sense? With all these miserable
distances and the praying mantises the only
people who ever look in. It isn't as if we
had to fear snoops or try to please them.
It's our own little place, for the time being.

JOHN:
I'm afraid Jack will see us before we see him.
And then out I'd go like a cloud,
lonely for my temporarily own disgusted little
flower and playmate, the best on the beach.

VIOLET:
You like to think you're involved with me
emotionally but what you're involved with

really is my lack of suitable clothes to
make an impression on the narrow world of
your narrow forehead. Some girls would say
you're stupid, but I'm not that patriotic.
No, you really are very sweet. Or at least
you have been. On occasion.

JOHN:
That was V day and the flags were out.

VIOLET:
I know you love me. *(They kiss.)* I didn't
know you loved me so much. What a magnifi-
cent gesture. I feel like a tube of hot
cement. What a lover, it's just like the
old days when the crows were in the corn
field and the rain was in the sky. You do
make me happy.

JOHN:
But it upsets me that you're never happy
for long. You know, Vi, I had big plans for
us. I thought we'd start a pet shop, a
little world of our own full of fondling and
loyalty and all the tiny things we've missed,
like ripples on a brook.

VIOLET:
You haven't talked this way since that after-
noon in Arlington Cemetery when the football
game was being broadcast over the car radio.
Come off it, you're no gangster of the sheets.
When I was little I promised myself not to
fall in love with anyone but the best polo
pony in the western world. Polo is a very

interesting sport, second only to duck fighting
in polls of national taste. What kind of lip-
stick did I have on?

JOHN:
Raspberry. Right?

VIOLET:
I knew you didn't love me.

JOHN:
You never knew. You don't know now. You'll
never be able to guess I don't and I'll
never give you any security on that score.
What do you want from life anyway? If you
weren't so elegant in all the intimate areas
where a man needs a lilting simplicity we
might have flamed like a rubber tire.

VIOLET:
You're cute as a pumpkin. I wonder what Jack
will look like. Do you think he'll still
love me? I hope so. If not, I may have been
premature in certain plans I've laid for your
so sustaining mouth.

JOHN:
You know it isn't very warm in here.

VIOLET:
I'd like to think about that remark but
inattention has become such a habit—
it's interesting and what you say is not.
Isn't that blue I see, poking its nose
over the picture frame falling down the
side of the moonlit mountain to the east

of the capitol? A screaming as of brakes.
I hope it's a train, I mean a boat, coming
in. Maybe Jack will swim down its gang-
plank into my absent arms like he used to
at parties. He was the living proof that
all women are members of the same sex.

JOHN:
So is everybody else.

VIOLET:
Well, I guess some
men are just more alive than others.

JOHN:
I didn't know you were so fond of this
male war bride. You never muttered his
name by mistake in my palpitating arms at
certain moments when the news of the world
was noisily grunting through its telescope.

VIOLET:
Not by mistake, I didn't. Like everyone
conceited, you are not without cause. You
are by popular consent the best lay within
these four walls, and that acclaim shall
never be denied you by tender me.

JOHN:
My own!

VIOLET:
Dearest of all forgotten ones!   *(They kiss.)*

JOHN:
Just think! Twice in one day. Our infatuation

is rearriving. What trouble it will arrange
to stir up in the next ten minutes between two
oh so troubled and disenchanted hearts!

    VIOLET:
Yes. Yes. The trouble I long for. The trouble
that keeps me, and shall continue to keep me,
from realizing what trouble is. Dear John.
   (They embrace.)

    JOHN:
Hey. What's this nasty piece of wood stuck
In your boobs?

    VIOLET:
Uh oh.

    JOHN:
Well?

    VIOLET:
It's a letter, a letter from Jack.

    JOHN:
Well what are you carrying it around for?
Haven't you read it yet?

    VIOLET:
Uh! *(She slaps him.)*

    JOHN:
How come you never showed me this?

    VIOLET:
You were never married to him.

JOHN:

When I think of the two of us, frail in our
affections, stranded on this planet of incessant
communication like gophers in their sweet-nosed
paralysis, or more similar to lovers who are very,
very sunburned! I marvel that we ever found it
possible or desirable to raise our lazy heads
from opposite ends of a gray fountain's inter-
section with the regimented air in order to just
say "Are you having fun?" to the dear person for
whom we are preparing, with passionately efficient
distraction, the deepest hurt, the one we did the
sweetly sweaty and individual push-ups and cold
creamings for, through the years. Doesn't it make
you marvel at human ambition? Is that a tear?

VIOLET:

Not on your life, you silly ass.
You can read the letter, don't carry on. No,
maybe you better not. It is my favorite letter.

JOHN:

Because, like all
sentimental women past their real gift-to-the-
world days, you're in love with your husband.
   (She dives for him. He grabs and pinions her.)

JOHN:

You want to toss me for who'll beat up whom?

VIOLET:

Oh read the damned thing!
   *(She breaks away from him and goes to the sculpture. During the letter-reading
   she drapes herself on it as if it represented the absent Jack to her.)*

JOHN:

I don't know if I'm well dressed enough. Where did
I put that rhinestone lavallière I stole from the
fairy at the ballet opening? Sit down, you silly
slut. You're not grappling with a stranger. One
bite out of you and Jack won't know you from an
ancient Kabuki.

VIOLET:

My hero! You're right out of a Noh play, aren't
you? Prince Jasmine Jock, himself.

JOHN:

Oh boy, this is great. *(Reads:)*

*Don't ever expect me to forget that moment of
brilliance when your blue eyes lit the train station
like a camera shutter. Your smile was like pink
crinoline going through a ringer. Seventeen trains
seemed to arrive and to bruisingly depart before I
caught my breath sufficiently to ask you for a match.
And then your perfume hit me like Niagara Falls.*

Asked you for a match? What
a relationship! Did he darn your aprons, too?
Get this. *(Reads:)*

*The pressure of being away from you is sometimes more
than even the scenery can bear, and it is alarmingly
brazen in piling snow over leaves and dark trunks lying
across roads where the push of centuries is like a
cymbal crashing in the roots of your hair. But I keep
on dreaming of you whether awake or asleep as they say
in songs, an azure dream. When I wake up, and I wake
up every time I think of you, my prick presses against*

my belly like a log of foreboding, and I'm afraid that
I'll die before I feel that thing that you are that
nobody else is to my body, like a trembling insight
into myself and the world I can't have. A train just
went by covered with icy fir trees. The sky is white.
I cry at night sometimes with my prick tangled in the
sheets—wishing it would go away and find you and leave
me alone in my, in this lousy southern country where
it's colder in the winter than it ever is in the cold
countries. But all I do is bitch and what I mean is
I love you.

He has a funny style, doesn't he ? It seems like a pose
but it must be that he isn't used to writing. He
wasn't a journalist or anything, was he? They're
sometimes very awkward. I see now; you were hiding
it from embarrassment!

    VIOLET:

I know it's enough for you that you amuse yourself,
so I won't complain of my own feelings. I do think I
despise you, but not as much as you would wish, or
I would wish. It's impossible that I could have
lived in precisely this airy derangement for this time
if any irony of yours could touch me deeply. It's not
that I love Jack! I hate my life.

    JOHN:

Princess Lonelyhearts.

    VIOLET:

Well let's not stop camping. We haven't seen the last
of each other, not us, not Little-Dimity-Head-Felt and
Bouncing-Broad-Britches. There's a tear left in this
magnificent vista yet. Just don't rust the pipes,

darling, and don't bump yourself tripping over the
arbutus. It's that green stuff with the velvet smile
that whines.

JOHN:
Dear god, I think that iron gate I put up as a weather
vane is creaking. An angel must be arriving.
Who do you suppose it could be?

VIOLET:
Well, one thing we have in common: we're both
    (primping)
beautiful people.

JOHN:
Yes, like a couple of cesspools.

VIOLET:
One season you're tan, you're happy, you're lying
beside an ocean, the hedges are shrinking with an
opium specific,

JOHN:
the next you're losing weight, you're cold, you're
getting bald, the floors are sealed against the
grovelling handclasp you extend into the bedrooms,
underneath the mezzanine.

VIOLET:
And when lust tries to make itself tangible but ends
up as the plot of your favorite silent movie over rye
and water under a slippery overhead mist, you want
that stranger you always awaited to hurry up, the
one you told everybody was an old friend who'd be
along in a minute.

JOHN:

A merchandise man from Chicago?

VIOLET:

No,
maybe an opera star who's retired for love.

(They retire offstage amorously. JACK *enters and stands silently looking around.* VIOLET *and* JOHN *re-enter with a certain post-coitus detachment from each other. After a pause:)*

JOHN:

Are you going to introduce me to the gentleman?

VIOLET:

Oh Jack! My Jackson!
why did you leave me?
Since you left I've had
to sell the flute and the
bathtub. And my voice
just froze. I'll never again
sing the popular songs
you composed while you were
on. Don't look at my fingernails.

JACK:

I've come a long way for your sake,
my back all decorated like this
and my feet covered with mold. Do
you know why they had to put fire
under my lids?

JOHN:
He *is* like his letters!

VIOLET:
Shut up.

JACK:
When we first went
riding, how like dashing Cossacks!
It was easy then to dress in scarlet.
I sat my mount prettily and hacked
babies and old women with a song
on my breast—I even let my eyebrows
grow! and with the gold braid and all
I frightened myself. There were sweet
times and we weren't too drunk to
appreciate them. Lovely ladies loved
us, like useful flowers. And as I say
my color was good. I had a beautiful horse.
Why, I thought of myself as
Eric's son, Lief, going towards
the moon with a world behind me
and a lot of blood to get off my
chest. I wanted to bellow the green
and black waves flat and then
cleave my way like an iceberg! I was
good and I knew it. I hadn't laid
them all low for nothing: women
and villages, coasts of islands
twice as big as Iceland. And didn't
they all squat when I frowned, even
my bad old father ? But something
went wrong. One minute I was lord of
all I surveyed, and the next I knew
that I'd be beaten—that I'd better
go back to my easy throne, and leave

this virgin land I'd first laid
heavy hands upon. That was a
retreat! how I cried to shove off
from that rich tough land, my
kind of country! and go home.
What was it that beat me? The land,
the air, the sun, all bigger than the
gods intended me to own? I yearned after it,
and it grew like a spiral as I thought
through the years of my Vinland the Good.
    (VIOLET *claps her hand over* JOHN's *mouth.*)
Or if I was the
Admiral, bossing a bothersome crew
and pretending a good deal of confidence,
when suddenly there was a hint of glory!
I didn't believe it, just because the
seaweed looked like fresh grass; I knew
I might be feverish and I didn't want to
be taken in, but there was something in the
air—a sweetness like finding a ruby when
you were looking for a baseball—and at
the same time I was scared at not knowing,
it was mine and I hadn't planned for it,
I wasn't strong enough, and anyone could
knock me down, all those others who wanted
everything as much as I did.

    JOHN:
Do I wake or sleep?

    VIOLET:
I don't know.
I'm beginning to think I'm the one who's
been away all along. And still am.

    JACK:
So I spent most of my time

wondering when bullets, mortars, and
bombs were going to find out where
my courage ended and this cowardice—
oh intuition, I'm not on trial am I?—
began. Finally a sniper in a tree
on the edge of the Pacific's
exciting waters—an oriental with
lots of time for meditation—
saw me clearly. At the right moment.
It was time, you see, not
topographical like Achilles' heel.
I was thinking of myself as heir
to the Mississippi. My thoughts moved
to De Soto—whose wouldn't? And
that was when I was spotted, naked
as the beach, caught within a few feet
of safety. Have you ever thought
about men like him—who could
have been emperors? I fell like a
sail, relaxed, with no surprise.
And here I am.

    VIOLET:
By default, you mean.

    JOHN:
Pardon me, I've got to take a terrific shit.

    VIOLET:
You may as well put your pants on
before you come back.
    (JOHN *goes rear and dresses.*)

    JACK:
Oh Violet!

VIOLET:
Now don't say anything you don't mean.
Just go on with the news bulletin. We're all
terribly interested in the outside world here.

JACK:
Well, if that's the way you feel. Who is
that anyway?

VIOLET:
A jazz musician named Lenny.

JACK:
He's billed as John under the buzzer in the hall.
Or is that another one?

VIOLET:
He's the boarder.

JACK:
The boarder?

VIOLET:
A boarder. You're looking handsome.

JACK:
Bunny!
    (They kiss fondly.)
What's he doing? Who *is* he?
    (She pulls away, withdrawing from him.)

VIOLET:
Children wade on the receding shingle
    (staring off)
gaunt in their practiced grace. Mature,

they ape their elders and cavort like
pogo sticks in the advancing foam.
Where well-mannered aeroplanes and autos
serenely sail, on the yellow sand, children
ignore their own innocence. They've taken it all
in, and know how they want their backs broken.
   (Then she faces him bitterly.)

   JACK:
I know all about the attractive distances and
the distraction that's more elegant than a knife.

   VIOLET:
Never mind the rabbits and tears. You're
just as ruthless as anyone else.

   JACK:
I thought
I'd want to play cards all night when I got home.
Listen, I know I'm stupid, I think for weeks
about things other people read in the newspaper.

   VIOLET:
You may be dumb, but it makes you clever
because you know it.

   JACK:
But I've been away.

   VIOLET:
All those letters, so beautiful . . .

   JACK:
I've been away,
that's all, I've just been away.

VIOLET:
. . . designed to upset
me sufficiently that I wouldn't be able to stop
whining about your absence until I heard the hoot
of the steamer bringing you back.

JACK:
It's still my life . . .

VIOLET:
Fortunately I've always had a very strong sense
of responsibility for the happiness of others.

JACK:
You're still in it.

VIOLET:
I'm a veritable Florence
Nightingale of the heart, or as one of your old friends
once remarked, "She has a bit of the good-hearted madam
in her." You see, you haven't asked me the right
questions.

JACK:
Am I looking handsome?

VIOLET:
Why don't you ask
me if my slip fits?

JACK:
Has he been staying here?

VIOLET:
Or if the steam-fitters union still meets for

its annual picnic in Lewisohn Stadium?
(JOHN *enters clothed.*)

JOHN:
Well, has my little Cio-Cio San told
the nasty Naval officer to scram?

JACK:
I'd like to have a word with you.

JOHN:
Let's have lunch together after you've found
yourself a job. I'm writing a novel your firm
may find itself interested in.
(VIOLET *turns to* JOHN.)

VIOLET:
I wish you'd
go away and stay away. All you've done is kept me
looking out windows, wondering what things were
really like. Get out!
(*But she throws herself into* JOHN's *arms and cries.*)

JOHN:
There, there.
(*He looks over her head at* JACK.)
What have you done to my poor baby to confuse her?
Why didn't you send us a telegram to expect you?
It was quite a shock to see you. I never saw you before,
so you can imagine how it's tested my equanimity.

JACK:
Shock! I come home to find you both in your
underwear in this place that looks like the
landscape outside a bottle factory, and you ask
me why I'm not more considerate of the woman who's
been eating my brain for years in the salt mines

of the heart, its panic? That's where all the wars
rage, you know. That's where all the despatches
come from. It's never a matter of killing, it's
a matter of suffering, it starts blowing up.
I want her, that's all, I want her breasts
leaning into my armpit against shop windows on
Sundays, I want the empty smell of her flesh
in the morning when she's gotten up to go to
the bathroom, I want her whole open valley
breathing noisily when we're drunk in the wet
mist of dawn as the pennants begin to stripe
themselves and the wind whines towards the
suburbs. You can't have her.

JOHN:
You're wrong.
She wants me, because she's interested enough
to hurt me. Life went to the trouble of putting
me here in these old but well-worn clothes
that've seen better days and better hers
and never even wanted to go away and get fixed up.
You've got a claim on it, but I've got it.
These things don't happen temporarily.

VIOLET:
I love you.
  (Against his neck.)

JACK:
What did I do wrong? What's happened to me? It's
like coming onto the stage, sitting down at the piano,
and finding no orchestra there! Why feel guilty, if
what I've done doesn't mean anything, if what I've said
doesn't move you? I held you in my heart, like a charm—

JOHN:
I suppose I'm the snake-in-the-grass but
I can't say I'm sorry. Someone has to smile

at her as she comes back from the bathroom.
Do you think everything can stay the same,
like a photograph? What for?
(JACK *starts to exit slowly.*)

VIOLET:
I would like to fill a jungle
with elephants and gorillas and
boa constrictors. I would like
to fill the trees and waterfalls
with the blackness in me, so I
might be a bird of paradise.

It would be fun to break a bottle
of wine and have it turn to water.
Or shoot a clay pigeon and have it
go honk! honk! and lay an egg in
the marshes. I'd rather not be
a wedding guest.

If I were the sphinx I could lie
in the sun and stare at myself
with pure white eyes. When I smiled
airplanes would go off their courses.
I'd hold down the dark and say
sweet nothings to the palms.
(He takes her in his arms.)

JOHN:
Honey, I designed that costume for you.
You always look that way to me.
That's why I'm so mean.

(CURTAIN)

1953

ON RACHMANINOFF'S BIRTHDAY

Quick! a last poem before I go
off my rocker. Oh Rachmaninoff!
Onset, Massachusetts. Is it the fig-newton
playing the horn? Thundering windows
of hell, will your tubes ever break
into powder? Oh my palace of oranges,
junk shop, staples, umber, basalt;
I'm a child again when I was really
miserable, a grope pizzicato. My pocket
of rhinestone, yoyo, carpenter's pencil,
amethyst, hypo, campaign button,
is the room full of smoke? Shit
on the soup, let it burn. So it's back.
You'll never be mentally sober.

1953

TO MY DEAD FATHER

Don't call to me father
wherever you are I'm
still your little son
running through the dark

I couldn't do what you
say even if I could hear
your roses no longer grow
my heart's black as their

bed their dainty thorns
have become my face's
troublesome stubble you
must not think of flowers

And do not frighten my
blue eyes with hazel flecks
or thicken my lips when
I face my mirror don't ask

that I be other than your
strange son understanding
minor miracles not death
father I am alive! father

forgive the roses and me

1953

THE HUNTER

He set out and kept hunting
and hunting. Where, he thought
and thought, is the real chamois?
and can I kill it where it is?
He had brought with him only a dish
of pears. The autumn wind soared
above the trails where the drops
of the chamois led him further.
The leaves dropped around him
like pie-plates. The stars fell
one by one into his eyes and burnt.

There is a geography which holds
its hands just so far from the breast
and pushes you away, crying so.
He went on to strange hills where
the stones were still warm from feet,
and then on and on. There were clouds
at his knees, his eyelashes
had grown thick from the colds,
as the fur of the bear does
in winter. Perhaps, he thought, I am
asleep, but he did not freeze to death.

There were little green needles
everywhere. And then manna fell.
He knew, above all, that he was now
approved, and his strength increased.
He saw the world below him, brilliant
as a floor, and steaming with gold,
with distance. There were occasionally
rifts in the cloud where the face
of a woman appeared, frowning. He

had gone higher. He wore ermine.
He thought, why did I come? and then,
I have come to rule! The chamois came.

The chamois found him and they came
in droves to humiliate him. Alone,
in the clouds, he was humiliated.

1953

GRAND CENTRAL

The wheels are inside me thundering.
They do not churn me, they are inside.
They were not oiled, they burn
with friction and out of my eyes
comes smoke. Then the enormous bullets
streak towards me with their black tracers
and bury themselves deep in my muscles.
They won't be taken out, I can still
move. Now I am going to lie down
like an expanse of marble floor
covered with commuters and information:
it is my vocation, you believe that,
don't you? I don't have an American
body, I have an anonymous body, though
you can get to love it, if you love
the corpses of the Renaissance; I am
reconstructed from a model of poetry,
you see, and this might be a horseless
carriage, it might be but it is not,
it is riddled with bullets, am I.
And if they are not thundering into me
they are thundering across me, on
the way to some devastated island
where they will eat waffles with the
other Americans of American persuasion.
On rainy days I ache as if a train
were about to arrive, I switch my tracks.

During the noon-hour rush a friend
of mine took a letter carrier across
the catwalk underneath the dome
behind the enormous (wheels! wheels!)
windows which are the roof of the sun
and knelt inside my cathedral, mine
through pain! and the thundering went on.
He unzipped the messenger's trousers
and relieved him of his missile, hands

on the messenger's dirty buttocks,
the smoking muzzle in his soft blue mouth.
That is one way of dominating the terminal,
but I have not done that. It will be
my blood, I think, that dominates the trains.

1953

HOMOSEXUALITY

So we are taking off our masks, are we, and keeping
our mouths shut? as if we'd been pierced by a glance!

The song of an old cow is not more full of judgment
than the vapors which escape one's soul when one is sick;

so I pull the shadows around me like a puff
and crinkle my eyes as if at the most exquisite moment

of a very long opera, and then we are off!
without reproach and without hope that our delicate feet

will touch the earth again, let alone "very soon."
It is the law of my own voice I shall investigate.

I start like ice, my finger to my ear, my ear
to my heart, that proud cur at the garbage can

in the rain. It's wonderful to admire oneself
with complete candor, tallying up the merits of each

of the latrines. 14th Street is drunken and credulous,
53rd tries to tremble but is too at rest. The good

love a park and the inept a railway station,
and there are the divine ones who drag themselves up

and down the lengthening shadow of an Abyssinian head
in the dust, trailing their long elegant heels of hot air

crying to confuse the brave "It's a summer day,
and I want to be wanted more than anything else in the world."

1954

TO A POET

I am sober and industrious
and would be plain and plainer
for a little while

                until my rococo
self is more assured of its
distinction.
            So you do not like
my new verses, written in the
pages of Russian novels while I do
not brood over an orderly
childhood?
            You are angry
because I see the white-haired
genius of the painter more beautiful
than the stammering vivacity

                     of
your temperament. And yes,
it becomes more and more a matter
of black and white between us

and when the doctor comes to
me he says "No things but in ideas"
or it is overheard
                in the public
square, now that I am off my couch.

1954

AUS EINEM APRIL

We dust the walls.
And of course we are weeping larks
falling all over the heavens with our shoulders clasped
in someone's armpits, so tightly! and our throats are full.
Haven't you ever fallen down at Christmas
and didn't it move everyone who saw you?
isn't that what the tree means? the pure pleasure
of making weep those whom you cannot move by your flights!
It's enough to drive one to suicide.
And the rooftops are falling apart like the applause

of rough, long-nailed, intimate, roughened-by-kisses, hands.
Fingers more breathless than a tongue laid upon the lips
in the hour of sunlight, early morning, before the mist rolls
in from the sea; and out there everything is turbulent and green.

1954

ON RACHMANINOFF'S BIRTHDAY

I am so glad that Larry Rivers made a
statue of me

and now I hear that my penis is on all
the statues of all the young sculptors who've
seen it

instead of the Picasso no-penis shep-
herd and its influence—for presence is
better than absence, if you love excess.

Oh now it is that all this music tumbles
round me which was once considered muddy

and today surrounds this ambiguity of
our tables and our typewriter paper, more
nostalgic than a disease,

soft as one's character, melancholy as
one's attractiveness,

offering the pernicious advice of dreams.
Is it too late for this?

I am what people make of me—if they
can and when they will. My difficulty is
readily played—like a rhapsody, or a fresh
house.

1954

EPIGRAM FOR JOE

Here is the edge of the water where
the delicate crabs drift like shells;
stick in your purple toe "I've been swimming
for hours, it's freezing!" and is it,
with all the salt falling like
a fountain across your mottled flesh,
each curling hair unguently draped by
the shivering sun, pushed by short breezes
into a molding for your hot heart, a wire
basket. And where the sands sting you
they gleam like matchsticks in the noon.
You are standing in the doorway on the
green threshhold while it licks feet
that are burning to spread and flutter.

1954

MEDITATIONS IN AN EMERGENCY

Am I to become profligate as if I were a blonde? Or religious as if I were French?

Each time my heart is broken it makes me feel more adventurous (and how the same names keep recurring on that interminable list!), but one of these days there'll be nothing left with which to venture forth.

Why should I share you? Why don't you get rid of someone else for a change?

I am the least difficult of men. All I want is boundless love.

Even trees understand me! Good heavens, I lie under them, too, don't I? I'm just like a pile of leaves.

However, I have never clogged myself with the praises of pastoral life, nor with nostalgia for an innocent past of perverted acts in pastures. No. One need never leave the confines of New York to get all the greenery one wishes—I can't even enjoy a blade of grass unless I know there's a subway handy, or a record store or some other sign that people do not totally *regret* life. It is more important to affirm the least sincere; the clouds get enough attention as it is and even they continue to pass. Do they know what they're missing? Uh huh.

My eyes are vague blue, like the sky, and change all the time; they are indiscriminate but fleeting, entirely specific and disloyal, so that no one trusts me. I am always looking away. Or again at something after it has given me up. It makes me restless and that makes me unhappy, but I cannot keep them still. If only I had grey, green, black, brown, yellow eyes; I would stay at home and do something. It's not that I'm curious. On the contrary, I am bored but it's my duty to be attentive, I am needed by things as the sky must be above the earth. And lately, so great has *their* anxiety become, I can spare myself little sleep.

Now there is only one man I love to kiss when he is unshaven. Heterosexuality! you are inexorably approaching. (How discourage her?)

St. Serapion, I wrap myself in the robes of your whiteness which is like midnight in Dostoevsky. How am I to become a legend, my dear? I've tried love, but that hides you in the bosom of another and I am always springing forth from it like the lotus—the ecstasy of always bursting forth! (but one must not be distracted by it!) or like a hyacinth, "to keep the filth of life away," yes, there, even in the heart, where the filth is pumped in and slanders and pollutes and determines. I will my will, though I may become famous for a mysterious vacancy in that department, that greenhouse.

Destroy yourself, if you don't know!

It is easy to be beautiful; it is difficult to appear so. I admire you, beloved, for the trap you've set. It's like a final chapter no one reads because the plot is over.

"Fanny Brown is run away—scampered off with a Cornet of Horse; I do love that little Minx, & hope She may be happy, tho' She has vexed me by this Exploit a little too. —Poor silly Cecchina! or F:B: as we used to call her. —I wish She had a good Whipping and 10,000 pounds." —Mrs. Thrale.

I've got to get out of here. I choose a piece of shawl and my dirtiest suntans. I'll be back, I'll re-emerge, defeated, from the valley; you don't want me to go where you go, so I go where you don't want me to. It's only afternoon, there's a lot ahead. There won't be any mail downstairs. Turning, I spit in the lock and the knob turns.

1954

TO THE MOUNTAINS IN NEW YORK

Yes! yes! yes! I've decided,
I'm letting my flock run around,
I'm dropping my pastoral pretensions!
and leaves don't fall into a little halo
on my tanned and worried head.
Let the houses fill up with dirt.
My master died in my heart.
On the molten streets of New York
the master put up signs of my death.
I love this hairy city.
It's wrinkled like a detective story
and noisy and getting fat and smudged
lids hood the sharp hard black eyes.
America's wandering away from me
in a dream of pine trees and clouds
of pubic dreams of the world at my feet.
The moon comes out: languorous
in spite of everything, towards all
its expectancy rides a slow white horse.
I walk watching, tripping, alleys
open and fall around me like footsteps
of a newly shod horse treading the
marble staircases of the palace
and the light screams of the nobility
oblige invisible bayonets. All
night I sit on the outspread knees
of addicts; their kindness
makes them talk like whores to
the sun as it moves me hysterically
forward. The subway shoots onto a ramp
overlooking the East River, the towers!
the minarets! The bridge. I'm lost.

There's no way back to the houses
filled with dirt. My master died
in my heart on the molten streets.

2

Everyone is drinking and falling
and the sour smiles of the wheels
and the curses of ambitious love.
I remember Moscow
I remember two herdsmen in fur caps
and they were lying down together
in the snow of their natural ferocity
which warded off the wolves.
But now no kisses reassure the animals
of my tent, and they wander drunkenly away
and I wander drunkenly here, clouded,
and I see no face to follow down the streets
through the gates of a great city
I was building to house the myth of my love.
I take a flowery drop of gin upon my tongue
and it receives the flaming sibilance
of the Volga. I am murmuring
past my own banks, rushing, floundering and black
at last, into the cleft of the filth.
My head is hot here in the snow and I dart
rebellious looks into the severely hidden
bootless snow. My own youth has narrowed
like a knife which cures the pleasures of life.

I shall never return! though I twist, come back,
grow pale, as the receding waves seem to lick the shore.
I cannot give myself now, I can only rush

towards you, engulf you, and pour forth!
The moon is desirous of detaining me, you,
but you are gone, and I follow.

     3
I feel the earth pulsing against my heart.
They call me The Dirt Eater. The Gambler.
I can't rise, I'm so filthy! so heavy!
at last I have my full stench, I've rediscovered
you. That's why you went away, isn't it?
I could have stayed forever in your arms.
But then I'd have become you. Now I've become the earth!
You died, and the tempestuous blue of my eyes
filled the sails of your funeral barque
which, I remember, was filled with walnuts.
It is raining. Shall I grow trees or flowers?

1954

MAYAKOVSKY

1

My heart's aflutter!
I am standing in the bath tub
crying. Mother, mother
who am I? If he
will just come back once
and kiss me on the face
his coarse hair brush
my temple, it's throbbing!

then I can put on my clothes
I guess, and walk the streets.

2

I love you. I love you,
but I'm turning to my verses
and my heart is closing
like a fist.

Words! be
sick as I am sick, swoon,
roll back your eyes, a pool,

and I'll stare down
at my wounded beauty
which at best is only a talent
for poetry.

Cannot please, cannot charm or win
what a poet!
and the clear water is thick

with bloody blows on its head.
I embraced a cloud,
but when I soared
it rained.

3

That's funny! there's blood on my chest
oh yes, I've been carrying bricks
what a funny place to rupture!
and now it is raining on the ailanthus
as I step out onto the window ledge
the tracks below me are smoky and
glistening with a passion for running
I leap into the leaves, green like the sea

4

Now I am quietly waiting for
the catastrophe of my personality
to seem beautiful again,
and interesting, and modern.

The country is grey and
brown and white in trees,
snows and skies of laughter
always diminishing, less funny
not just darker, not just grey.

It may be the coldest day of
the year, what does he think of
that? I mean, what do I? And if I do,
perhaps I am myself again.

1954

IN THE MOVIES

Out of the corner of my eyes
a tear of revulsion sighs,
it's the point of intersection a foot in front of me,
I call it my cornea, my Muse.
I hurl myself there—at whatever fatal flowery flourish!
flower? flower?
if that face is flourishing, it's toes of tin!
Well, but there is a face there, a ravine of powder and gasps,
I can see it, I must caress it.
I give it one of my marine caresses since it is inferior, petulant.
And the clear water of my head pours over that face.

Flowers. Flowers.
Just because the day is as long and white as a camel
you'll see my head leaning against this masseur of a seat
and the blood in my pants mounts to the stars
as I ponder the silver square.

Flowers. Flowers,
every afternoon at one, why not caress the wind
which passes from the air conditioning to my seat?
as the waters underneath Times Square
pour through my eyes onto the silver screen.
I'm here, pale and supple as a horse-shrine.

Ushers! ushers!
do you seek me with your lithe flashlights?
enveloping me like the controlled current of the air?
There seems to be a ghost up there,
brushing off his gems and plumes.
It's a great feathery candle glowing in the rain
of my fine retrieving gaze,
the large feathered prick that impaled me in the grass.
It was an organ that announced a certain destiny.
And as the plumes flutter in the current they spell out *****

but I don't believe my eyes, it's only a ghost's habit.
I bought a ticket so I could be alone. With the plumes.
With the ushers.
With my own prick,
and with my death written in smoke
outside this theatre where I receive my mail.
Guts? my gut is full of water, like the River Jordan.

The pressure of my boredom is uplifting and cool,
I feel its familiar hands on my buttocks.
And we depend on the screen for accompaniment,
its mirrors
its music
because I've left everything behind but a leaf
and now a dark hand lifts that from my thighs
(out of the corner of my eyes
a tear of revulsion sighs).
No, I've never been in a cotton field in South Carolina.
My head is lost between your purple lips.
Your teeth glitter like the Aurora Borealis.

Cerise trees are plunging through my veins
and not one lumberjack is drowned in my giant flesh.
This stranger collects me like a sea-story
and now I am part of his marine slang.
Waves break in the theatre
and flame finds a passage through the stormy straits of my lips.

In my hands a black cloud of soft winds
pulses forth the error of my blood and my body,
like a poem written in blackface,
his flower opens and I press my face into the dahlialike mirror
whose lips press mine with the grandeur of a torrent,
it is flooding the cleft of my rocklike face
which burns with the anguish of a plaster beast!
I am said to have the eyes of a camelopard
and the lips of an oriole,

it's my movie reputation—
so now you've found my germinal spontaneity
and you are my voyage to Africa.

I love your naked storms.
I contemplate you with the profound regard of a scriptwriter.
The serene horse of your forgetfulness is a crater
in which I bathe the pride of my race,
as we splash away the afternoon
in the movies
and in the mountains.

Reflect a moment on the flesh in which you're mired:
I'm the white heron of your darkness,
I'm the ghost of a tribal chief killed in battle
and I bear proudly the slit nose of your victories.

Suffer my cornea to adopt a verbal blueness,
for you are the sick prince of my cerise innovations,
and my seriousness.
I bear you mirrors
and I kiss the sill of your porcelain fountain,
dreaming midst the flamingo plumes of your penis.

Seized by flames!
seized by winds!
sea of my sex and your red domination!
(red is for my heart and for the wind of my islands)
which envelops this insect, my self,
and salutes your loins
as the shadowy horses increase
and I pale with butterfly aspirations.

Do you feel the hairs that fill my mouth like aigrettes,
as moss fills the stone with longing no hands can tear away?
do you feel your sword imbedded in the legendary rock?
the repose of rivers,

the source of warriors,
warriors of the stars which are my sighs
and my sighs are black
because my blood is black with your love,
the love of the jungle for its secret pools.

We take the silver way along the rocks
and with my head upon your chocolate breast
the screen is again a horizon of blood.
The drapes flutter around us like cement.
In your drowning caresses I walk the sea.
I am gilded with your sweat
and your hair smells of herbs
from which I do not care to peer.

If love is born from this projection in the golden beehive like a swan,
I love you.
I am lighting up the evening which is yours,
I implore you;
and the smoke of my death will have blown away by now,
as my ghosts are laid along your glittering teeth.

1954

MUSIC

If I rest for a moment near The Equestrian
pausing for a liver sausage sandwich in the Mayflower Shoppe,
that angel seems to be leading the horse into Bergdorf's
and I am naked as a table cloth, my nerves humming.
Close to the fear of war and the stars which have disappeared.
I have in my hands only 35¢, it's so meaningless to eat!
and gusts of water spray over the basins of leaves
like the hammers of a glass pianoforte. If I seem to you
to have lavender lips under the leaves of the world,
     I must tighten my belt.
It's like a locomotive on the march, the season
     of distress and clarity
and my door is open to the evenings of midwinter's
lightly falling snow over the newspapers.
Clasp me in your handkerchief like a tear, trumpet
of early afternoon! in the foggy autumn.
As they're putting up the Christmas trees on Park Avenue
I shall see my daydreams walking by with dogs in blankets,
put to some use before all those coloured lights come on!
     But no more fountains and no more rain,
     and the stores stay open terribly late.

1954

TO JOHN ASHBERY

I can't believe there's not
another world where we will sit
and read new poems to each other
high on a mountain in the wind.
You can be Tu Fu, I'll be Po Chü-i
and the Monkey Lady'll be in the moon,
smiling at our ill-fitting heads
as we watch snow settle on a twig.
Or shall we be really gone?   this
is not the grass I saw in my youth!
and if the moon, when it rises
tonight, is empty—a bad sign,
meaning "You go, like the blossoms."

1954

FOR GRACE, AFTER A PARTY

You do not always know what I am feeling.
Last night in the warm spring air while I was
blazing my tirade against someone who doesn't
interest
             me, it was love for you that set me
afire,
             and isn't it odd? for in rooms full of
strangers my most tender feelings
                                              writhe and
bear the fruit of screaming. Put out your hand,
isn't there
             an ashtray, suddenly, there? beside
the bed? And someone you love enters the room
and says wouldn't
                         you like the eggs a little
different today?
                         And when they arrive they are
just plain scrambled eggs and the warm weather
is holding.

1954

POEM

I watched an armory combing its bronze bricks
and in the sky there were glistening rails of milk.
Where had the swan gone, the one with the lame back?

       Now mounting the steps
       I enter my new home full
       of grey radiators and glass
       ashtrays full of wool.

Against the winter I must get a samovar
embroidered with basil leaves and Ukranian mottos
to the distant sound of wings, painfully anti-wind,

       a little bit of the blue
       summer air will come back
       as the steam chuckles in
       the monster's steamy attack

and I'll be happy here and happy there, full
of tea and tears. I don't suppose I'll ever get
to Italy, but I have the terrible tundra at least.

       My new home will be full
       of wood, roots and the like,
       while I pace in a turtleneck
       sweater, repairing my bike.

I watched the palisades shivering in the snow
of my face, which had grown preternaturally pure.
Once I destroyed a man's idea of himself to have him.

       If I'd had a samovar then
       I'd have made him tea
       and as hyacinths grow from
       a pot he would love me

and my charming room of tea cosies full of dirt
which is why I must travel, to collect the leaves.
O my enormous piano, you are not like being outdoors

      though it is cold and you
      are made of fire and wood!
      I lift your lid and mountains
      return, that I am good.

The stars blink like a hairnet that was dropped
on a seat and now it is lying in the alley behind
the theater where my play is echoed by dying voices.

      I am really a woodcarver
      and my words are love
      which willfully parades in
      its room, refusing to move.

1954

POEM

to James Schuyler

There I could never be a boy,
though I rode like a god when the horse reared.
At a cry from mother I fell to my knees!
there I fell, clumsy and sick and good,
though I bloomed on the back of a frightened black mare
who had leaped windily at the start of a leaf
and she never threw me.

I had a quick heart
and my thighs clutched her back.
I loved her fright, which was against me
into the air! and the diamond white of her forelock
which seemed to smart with thoughts as my heart smarted with life!
and she'd toss her head with the pain
and paw the air and champ the bit, as if I were Endymion
and she, moonlike, hated to love me.

All things are tragic
when a mother watches!
and she wishes upon herself
the random fears of a scarlet soul, as it breathes in and out
and nothing chokes, or breaks from triumph to triumph!

I knew her but I could not be a boy,
for in the billowing air I was fleet and green
riding blackly through the ethereal night
towards men's words which I gracefully understood,

and it was given to me
as the soul is given the hands
to hold the ribbons of life!
as miles streak by beneath the moon's sharp hooves
and I have mastered the speed and strength which is the armor of the world.

1954

TO THE HARBORMASTER

I wanted to be sure to reach you;
though my ship was on the way it got caught
in some moorings. I am always tying up
and then deciding to depart. In storms and
at sunset, with the metallic coils of the tide
around my fathomless arms, I am unable
to understand the forms of my vanity
or I am hard alee with my Polish rudder
in my hand and the sun sinking. To
you I offer my hull and the tattered cordage
of my will. The terrible channels where
the wind drives me against the brown lips
of the reeds are not all behind me. Yet
I trust the sanity of my vessel; and
if it sinks, it may well be in answer
to the reasoning of the eternal voices,
the waves which have kept me from reaching you.

1954

UNE JOURNÉE DE JUILLET

My back is peeling and the tar
melts underfoot as I cross the street.
Sweaty foreheads wipe on my shirt
as I pass. The sun hits a building
and shines off onto my face. The sun
licks my feet through my moccasins
as I feel my way along the asphalt.
The sun beams on my buttocks
as I outdistance the crowd. For a
moment I enter the cavernous vault
and its deadish cold. I suck off
every man in the Manhattan Storage &
Warehouse Co. Then, refreshed, again
to the streets! to the generous sun
and the vigorous heat of the city.

1955

AT THE OLD PLACE

Joe is restless and so am I, so restless.
Button's buddy lips frame "L G T TH O P?"
across the bar. "Yes!" I cry, for dancing's
my soul delight. (Feet! feet!) "Come on!"

Through the streets we skip like swallows.
Howard malingers. (Come on, Howard.) Ashes
malingers. (Come on, J.A.) Dick malingers.
(Come on, Dick.) Alvin darts ahead. (Wait up,
Alvin.) Jack, Earl and Someone don't come.

Down the dark stairs drifts the steaming cha-
cha-cha. Through the urine and smoke we charge
to the floor. Wrapped in Ashes' arms I glide.
(It's heaven!) Button lindys with me. (It's
heaven!) Joe's two-steps, too, are incredible,
and then a fast rhumba with Alvin, like skipping
on toothpicks. And the interminable intermissions,

we have them. Jack, Earl and Someone drift
guiltily in. "I knew they were gay
the minute I laid eyes on them!" screams John.
How ashamed they are of us!   we hope.

1955

NOCTURNE

There's nothing worse
than feeling bad and not
being able to tell you.
Not because you'd kill me
or it would kill you, or
we don't love each other.
It's space. The sky is grey
and clear, with pink and
blue shadows under each cloud.
A tiny airliner drops its
specks over the U N Building.
My eyes, like millions of
glassy squares, merely reflect.
Everything sees through me,
in the daytime I'm too hot
and at night I freeze; I'm
built the wrong way for the
river and a mild gale would
break every fiber in me.
Why don't I go east and west
instead of north and south?
It's the architect's fault.
And in a few years I'll be
useless, not even an office
building. Because you have
no telephone, and live so
far away; the Pepsi-Cola sign,
the seagulls and the noise.

1955

POEM

Johnny and Alvin are going home, are sleeping now
are fanning the air with breaths from the same bed.

The moon is covered with gauze and the laughs
are not in them. The boats honk and the barges heave

a little, so the river is moved by a faint breeze.
Where are the buses that would take them to another state?

standing on corners; a nurse waits with a purse
and a murderer escapes the detectives by taking a public

conveyance through the summer's green reflections.
There's too much lime in the world and not enough gin,

they gasp. The gentle are curious, but the curious
are not gentle. So the breaths come home and sleep.

1955

TO AN ACTOR WHO DIED

As the days go, and they go fast on this island
where the firs grow blue and the golden seaweed
clambers up the rocks, I think of you, and death
comes not, except a sea urchin's dropped and cracked

on the rocks and falling bird eats him to rise
more strongly into fog or luminous purple wind. So
to be used and rest, the spiny thing is empty, still
increasing decoration on the craggy slopes above

the barnacles. Lightly falls the grieving light
over the heel of Great Spruce Head Island, like cool
words turning their back on the bayness of the bay
and open water where the swell says heavy things

and smoothly to the nonreflective caves. Clover lies,
in its mauve decline, to the butterflies and bumblebees
and hummingbirds and hornets finding not their sucking
appetites attractive in its stirring dryness, robbed

out of succulence into fainting, rattling noise. Only
the child loves noise, your head is clear as a rock
in air above the fish hawk's habitual shriek at menace
already moving away, above the fish which will not leave the weir

once there as the tide has pulled them. The holy land
outside of nature nothing feeds, as rocks address no sun.

1955

THINKING OF JAMES DEAN

Like a nickelodeon soaring over the island from sea to bay,
two pots of gold, and the flushed effulgence of a sky Tiepolo
and Turner had compiled in vistavision. Each panoramic second, of
his death. The rainbows canceling each other out, between martinis

and the steak. To bed to dream, the moon invisibly scudding
under black-blue clouds, a stern Puritanical breeze pushing at
the house, to dream of roaches nibbling at my racing toenails,
great-necked speckled geese and slapping their proud heads

as I ran past. Morning. The first plunge in dolorous surf
and the brilliant sunlight declaring all the qualities of the world.
Like an ant, dragging its sorrows up and down the sand to find
a hiding place never, here where everything is guarded by dunes

or drifting. The sea is dark and smells of fish beneath its
silver surface. To reach the depths and rise, only in the sea;
the abysses of life, incessantly plunging not to rise to a face
of heat and joy again; habits of total immersion and the stance

victorious in death. And after hours of lying in nature, to nature,
and simulated death in the crushing waves, their shells and heart
pounding me naked on the shingle: had I died at twenty-four as he, but
in Boston, robbed of these suns and knowledges, a corpse more whole,

less deeply torn, less bruised and less alive, perhaps backstage
at the Brattle Theatre amidst the cold cream and the familiar lice
in my red-gold costume for a bit in *Julius Caesar*, would I be
smaller now in the vastness of light? a cork in the monumental

stillness of an eye-green trough, a sliver on the bleaching beach
to airplanes carried by the panting clouds to Spain. My friends
are roaming or listening to *La Bohème*. Precisely, the cold last swim
before the city flatters meanings of my life I cannot find,

squeezing me like an orange for some nebulous vitality, mourning
to the fruit ignorant of science in its hasty dying, kissing
its leaves and stem, exuding oils of Florida in the final glass of
pleasure. A leaving word in the sand, odor of tides: his name.

1955

MY HEART

I'm not going to cry all the time
nor shall I laugh all the time,
I don't prefer one "strain" to another.
I'd have the immediacy of a bad movie,
not just a sleeper, but also the big,
overproduced first-run kind. I want to be
at least as alive as the vulgar. And if
some aficionado of my mess says "That's
not like Frank!," all to the good! I
don't wear brown and grey suits all the time,
do I? No. I wear workshirts to the opera,
often. I want my feet to be bare,
I want my face to be shaven, and my heart—
you can't plan on the heart, but
the better part of it, my poetry, is open.

1955

TO THE FILM INDUSTRY IN CRISIS

Not you, lean quarterlies and swarthy periodicals
with your studious incursions toward the pomposity of ants,
nor you, experimental theatre in which Emotive Fruition
is wedding Poetic Insight perpetually, nor you,
promenading Grand Opera, obvious as an ear (though you
are close to my heart), but you, Motion Picture Industry,
it's you I love!

In times of crisis, we must all decide again and again whom we love.
And give credit where it's due: not to my starched nurse, who taught me
how to be bad and not bad rather than good (and has lately availed
herself of this information), not to the Catholic Church
which is at best an oversolemn introduction to cosmic entertainment,
not to the American Legion, which hates everybody, but to you,
glorious Silver Screen, tragic Technicolor, amorous Cinemascope,
stretching Vistavision and startling Stereophonic Sound, with all
your heavenly dimensions and reverberations and iconoclasms! To
Richard Barthelmess as the "tol'able" boy barefoot and in pants,
Jeanette MacDonald of the flaming hair and lips and long, long neck,
Sue Carroll as she sits for eternity on the damaged fender of a car
and smiles, Ginger Rogers with her pageboy bob like a sausage
on her shuffling shoulders, peach-melba-voiced Fred Astaire of the feet,
Eric von Stroheim, the seducer of mountain-climbers' gasping spouses,
the Tarzans, each and every one of you (I cannot bring myself to prefer
Johnny Weissmuller to Lex Barker, I cannot!), Mae West in a furry sled,
her bordello radiance and bland remarks, Rudolph Valentino of the moon,
its crushing passions, and moonlike, too, the gentle Norma Shearer,
Miriam Hopkins dropping her champagne glass off Joel McCrea's yacht
and crying into the dappled sea, Clark Gable rescuing Gene Tierney
from Russia and Allan Jones rescuing Kitty Carlisle from Harpo Marx,
Cornel Wilde coughing blood on the piano keys while Merle Oberon berates,
Marilyn Monroe in her little spike heels reeling through Niagara Falls,
Joseph Cotten puzzling and Orson Welles puzzled and Dolores del Rio
eating orchids for lunch and breaking mirrors, Gloria Swanson reclining,
and Jean Harlow reclining and wiggling, and Alice Faye reclining
and wiggling and singing, Myrna Loy being calm and wise, William Powell
in his stunning urbanity, Elizabeth Taylor blossoming, yes, to you

and to all you others, the great, the near-great, the featured, the extras
who pass quickly and return in dreams saying your one or two lines,
my love!
Long may you illumine space with your marvellous appearances, delays
and enunciations, and may the money of the world glitteringly cover you
as you rest after a long day under the kleig lights with your faces
in packs for our edification, the way the clouds come often at night
but the heavens operate on the star system. It is a divine precedent
you perpetuate! Roll on, reels of celluloid, as the great earth rolls on!

1955

ON SEEING LARRY RIVERS'
WASHINGTON CROSSING THE DELAWARE
AT THE MUSEUM OF MODERN ART

Now that our hero has come back to us
in his white pants and we know his nose
trembling like a flag under fire,
we see the calm cold river is supporting
our forces, the beautiful history.

To be more revolutionary than a nun
is our desire, to be secular and intimate
as, when sighting a redcoat, you smile
and pull the trigger. Anxieties
and animosities, flaming and feeding

on theoretical considerations and
the jealous spiritualities of the abstract,
the robot? they're smoke, billows above
the physical event. They have burned up.
See how free we are! as a nation of persons.

Dear father of our country, so alive
you must have lied incessantly to be
immediate, here are your bones crossed
on my breast like a rusty flintlock,
a pirate's flag, bravely specific

and ever so light in the misty glare
of a crossing by water in winter to a shore
other than that the bridge reaches for.
Don't shoot until, the white of freedom glinting
on your gun barrel, you see the general fear.

1955

94

RADIO

Why do you play such dreary music
on Saturday afternoon, when tired
mortally tired I long for a little
reminder of immortal energy?
                                          All
week long while I trudge fatiguingly
from desk to desk in the museum
you spill your miracles of Grieg
and Honegger on shut-ins.
                                Am I not
shut in too, and after a week
of work don't I deserve Prokofieff?

Well, I have my beautiful de Kooning
to aspire to. I think it has an orange
bed in it, more than the ear can hold.

                        1955

SLEEPING ON THE WING

Perhaps it is to avoid some great sadness,
as in a Restoration tragedy the hero cries "Sleep!
O for a long sound sleep and so forget it!"
that one flies, soaring above the shoreless city,
veering upward from the pavement as a pigeon
does when a car honks or a door slams, the door
of dreams, life perpetuated in parti-colored loves
and beautiful lies all in different languages.

Fear drops away too, like the cement, and you
are over the Atlantic. Where is Spain? where is
who? The Civil War was fought to free the slaves,
was it? A sudden down-draught reminds you of gravity
and your position in respect to human love. But
here is where the gods are, speculating, bemused.
Once you are helpless, you are free, can you believe
that? Never to waken to the sad struggle of a face?
to travel always over some impersonal vastness,
to be out of, forever, neither in nor for!

The eyes roll asleep as if turned by the wind
and the lids flutter open slightly like a wing.
The world is an iceberg, so much is invisible!
and was and is, and yet the form, it may be sleeping
too. Those features etched in the ice of someone
loved who died, you are a sculptor dreaming of space
and speed, your hand alone could have done this.
Curiosity, the passionate hand of desire. Dead,
or sleeping? Is there speed enough? And, swooping,
you relinquish all that you have made your own,
the kingdom of your self sailing, for you must awake
and breathe your warmth in this beloved image
whether it's dead or merely disappearing,
as space is disappearing and your singularity.

1955

JOSEPH CORNELL

Into a sweeping meticulously-
detailed disaster the violet
light pours. It's not a sky,
it's a room. And in the open
field a glass of absinthe is
fluttering its song of India.
Prairie winds circle mosques.

You are always a little too
young to understand. He is
bored with his sense of the
past, the artist. Out of the
prescient rock in his heart
he has spread a land without
flowers of near distances.

1955

[IT IS 1:55 IN CAMBRIDGE, PALE AND SPRING COOL,]

It is 1:55 in Cambridge, pale and spring cool,
it is. Evenings in Jim's Place with Jimmy
and listening to Lenya sing all day long. Yes,
I would like another beer and Bert Brecht is
a great poet, and Kurt Weill, he is a genius too.
Most of all it is a gift from Wystan, Germany,
when years ago Storm Troopers came close
as a knock on our doors before we met, as
terrifying as a game at recess when the bullies
were on the other side. And when they were on
our side it was worse. And gradually fearing
disappeared in knowing, another gift from Wystan,
though it too was worse, for there is no paying
on both sides. And now it is almost the last hour
of your visit, Jimmy, no more walks by the Charles
"the alluvial river" drifting through a town
that's pretty because it is so flat. No more
great decisions on titles and places, no more
too many drinks. Will those poems ever get
written? will our royalties from VISITING
ANGKOR VAT AND VIENNA really sustain us, in a
future that only yesterday seemed so literally
bright? Goodbye. At least we've written our ODE.
And elsewhere, as snows dirty, we'll sit
for long long days and talk and play the phonograph
and heat the coffee. And silent, go to a bar.

1956

POEM

"Two communities outside Birmingham, Alabama, are still searching for their dead."
———NEWS TELECAST

And tomorrow morning at 8 o'clock in Springfield, Massachusetts,
my oldest aunt will be buried from a convent.
Spring is here and I am staying here, I'm not going.
Do birds fly? I am thinking my own thoughts, who else's?

> When I die, don't come, I wouldn't want a leaf
> to turn away from the sun—it loves it there.
> There's nothing so spiritual about being happy
> but you can't miss a day of it, because it doesn't last.

So this is the devil's dance? Well I was born to dance.
It's a sacred duty, like being in love with an ape,
and eventually I'll reach some great conclusion, like assumption,
when at last I meet exhaustion in these flowers, go straight up.

1956

POEM

Instant coffee with slightly sour cream
in it, and a phone call to the beyond
which doesn't seem to be coming any nearer.
"Ah daddy, I wanna stay drunk many days"
on the poetry of a new friend
my life held precariously in the seeing
hands of others, their and my impossibilities.
Is this love, now that the first love
has finally died, where there were no impossibilities?

1956

RETURNING

Coming down the ladder
you can hardly remember the plane was like a rabbit
                        the air above the clouds
                        that settling into the earth
                was like diving onto the sea on your belly,
there are so many similarities you have forgotten.

Well, there are a lot of things you haven't forgotten,
walking through the waiting room you know you should go
to bed with everyone who looks at you because the war's not over,
no assurance yet that desire's an exaggeration
and you don't want anyone to turn out to be a ruined city, do you?

As Marilyn Monroe says, it's a responsibility being a sexual symbol,
and as everyone says, it's the property of a symbol to be sexual.
Who's confused? Dead citizen or survivor, it's only your cock or your ass.
They do what they can in gardens and parks,
                        in subway stations and latrines,
as boyscouts rub sticks together who've read the manual,
                        know what's expected of death.

1956

IN MEMORY OF MY FEELINGS

to Grace Hartigan

I

My quietness has a man in it, he is transparent
and he carries me quietly, like a gondola, through the streets.
He has several likenesses, like stars and years, like numerals.
My quietness has a number of naked selves,
so many pistols I have borrowed to protect myselves
from creatures who too readily recognize my weapons
and have murder in their heart!
                           though in winter
they are warm as roses, in the desert
taste of chilled anisette.
                   At times, withdrawn,
I rise into the cool skies
and gaze on at the imponderable world with the simple identification
of my colleagues, the mountains. Manfred climbs to my nape,
speaks, but I do not hear him,
                      I'm too blue.
An elephant takes up his trumpet,
money flutters from the windows of cries, silk stretching its mirror
across shoulder blades. A gun is "fired."
                       One of me rushes
to window #13 and one of me raises his whip and one of me
flutters up from the center of the track amidst the pink flamingoes,
and underneath their hooves as they round the last turn my lips
are scarred and brown, brushed by tails, masked in dirt's lust,
definition, open mouths gasping for the cries of the bettors for the lungs
of earth.
        So many of my transparencies could not resist the race!
Terror in earth, dried mushrooms, pink feathers, tickets,
a flaking moon drifting across the muddied teeth,
the imperceptible moan of covered breathing,
                           love of the serpent!
I am underneath its leaves as the hunter crackles and pants
and bursts, as the barrage balloon drifts behind a cloud
and animal death whips out its flashlight,
                      whistling

and slipping the glove off the trigger hand. The serpent's eyes
redden at sight of those thorny fingernails, he is so smooth!

My transparent selves
flail about like vipers in a pail, writhing and hissing
without panic, with a certain justice of response
and presently the aquiline serpent comes to resemble the Medusa.

   2

The dead hunting
and the alive, ahunted.

My father, my uncle,
my grand-uncle and the several aunts. My
grand-aunt dying for me, like a talisman, in the war,
before I had even gone to Borneo
her blood vessels rushed to the surface
and burst like rockets over the wrinkled
invasion of the Australians, her eyes aslant
like the invaded, but blue like mine.
An atmosphere of supreme lucidity,

humanism,
the mere existence of emphasis,

a rusted barge
painted orange against the sea
full of Marines reciting the Arabian ideas
which are a proof in themselves of seasickness
which is a proof in itself of being hunted.
A hit? *ergo* swim.

My 10   my 19,
my 9,   and the several years. My
12 years since they all died, philosophically speaking.
And now the coolness of a mind
like a shuttered suite in the Grand Hotel
where mail arrives for my incognito,

whose façade
has been slipping into the Grand Canal for centuries;
rockets splay over a *sposalizio*,

                                   fleeing into night
from their Chinese memories, and it is a celebration,
the trying desperately to count them as they die.
But who will stay to be these numbers
when all the lights are dead?

        3
The most arid stretch is often richest,
the hand lifting towards a fig tree from hunger
                                        digging
and there is water, clear, supple, or there
deep in the sand where death sleeps, a murmurous bubbling
proclaims the blackness that will ease and burn.
You preferred the Arabs? but they didn't stay to count
their inventions, racing into sands, converting themselves into
so many,
              embracing, at Ramadan, the tenderest effigies of
themselves with penises shorn by the hundreds, like a camel
ravishing a goat.
                    And the mountainous-minded Greeks could speak
of time as a river and step across it into Persia, leaving the pain
at home to be converted into statuary. I adore the Roman copies.
And the stench of the camel's spit I swallow,
and the stench of the whole goat. For we have advanced, France,
together into a new land, like the Greeks, where one feels nostalgic
for mere ideas, where truth lies on its deathbed like an uncle
and one of me has a sentimental longing for number,
as has another for the ball gowns of the Directoire and yet
another for "Destiny, Paris, destiny!"
                              or "Only a king may kill a king."

How many selves are there in a war hero asleep in names? under
a blanket of platoon and fleet, orderly. For every seaman
with one eye closed in fear and twitching arm at a sigh for Lord Nelson,
he is all dead; and now a meek subaltern writhes in his bedclothes

with the fury of a thousand, violating an insane mistress
who has only herself to offer his multitudes.
                                        Rising,
he wraps himself in the burnoose of memories against the heat of life
and over the sands he goes to take an algebraic position *in re*
a sun of fear shining not too bravely. He will ask himselves to
vote on fear before he feels a tremor,
                                as runners arrive from the mountains
bearing snow, proof that the mind's obsolescence is still capable
of intimacy. His mistress will follow him across the desert
like a goat, towards a mirage which is something familiar about
one of his innumerable wrists,
                                and lying in an oasis one day,
playing catch with coconuts, they suddenly smell oil.

        4
Beneath these lives
the ardent lover of history hides,
                        tongue out
leaving a globe of spit on a taut spear of grass
and leaves off rattling his tail a moment
to admire this flag.
                I'm looking for my Shanghai Lil.
Five years ago, enamored of fire-escapes, I went to Chicago,
an eventful trip: the fountains! the Art Institute, the Y
for both sexes, absent Christianity.
                        At 7, before Jane
was up, the copper lake stirred against the sides
of a Norwegian freighter; on the deck a few dirty men,
tired of night, watched themselves in the water
as years before the German prisoners on the Prinz Eugen
dappled the Pacific with their sores, painted purple
by a Naval doctor.
                Beards growing, and the constant anxiety
over looks. I'll shave before she wakes up. Sam Goldwyn

spent $2,000,000 on Anna Sten, but Grushenka left America.
One of me is standing in the waves, an ocean bather,
or I am naked with a plate of devils at my hip.

        Grace
to be born and live as variously as possible. The conception
of the masque barely suggests the sordid identifications.
I am a Hittite in love with a horse. I don't know what blood's
in me I feel like an African prince I am a girl walking downstairs
in a red pleated dress with heels I am a champion taking a fall
I am a jockey with a sprained ass-hole I am the light mist
        in which a face appears
and it is another face of blonde I am a baboon eating a banana
I am a dictator looking at his wife I am a doctor eating a child
and the child's mother smiling I am a Chinaman climbing a mountain
I am a child smelling his father's underwear I am an Indian
sleeping on a scalp
     and my pony is stamping in the birches,
and I've just caught sight of the *Niña,* the *Pinta* and the *Santa Maria.*
     What land is this, so free?
        I watch
the sea at the back of my eyes, near the spot where I think
in solitude as pine trees groan and support the enormous winds,
they are humming *L'Oiseau de feu!*
      They look like gods, these whitemen,
and they are bringing me the horse I fell in love with on the frieze.

  5
And now it is the serpent's turn.
I am not quite you, but almost, the opposite of visionary.
You are coiled around the central figure,
        the heart
that bubbles with red ghosts, since to move is to love
and the scrutiny of all things is syllogistic,
the startled eyes of the dikdik, the bush full of white flags
fleeing a hunter,

which is our democracy
                              but the prey
is always fragile and like something, as a seashell can be
a great Courbet, if it wishes. To bend the ear of the outer world.
                              When you turn your head
can you feel your heels, undulating? that's what it is
to be a serpent. I haven't told you of the most beautiful things
in my lives, and watching the ripple of their loss disappear
along the shore, underneath ferns,
                              face downward in the ferns
my body, the naked host to my many selves, shot
by a guerrilla warrior or dumped from a car into ferns
which are themselves *journalières.*
                              The hero, trying to unhitch his parachute,
stumbles over me. It is our last embrace.
                              And yet
I have forgotten my loves, and chiefly that one, the cancerous
statue which my body could no longer contain,
                              against my will
                              against my love
become art,
                    I could not change it into history
and so remember it,
                    and I have lost what is always and everywhere
present, the scene of my selves, the occasion of these ruses,
which I myself and singly must now kill
                              and save the serpent in their midst.

                                        1956

[AND LEAVING IN A GREAT SMOKY FURY]

And leaving in a great smoky fury
of his loved ones, he sailed
backwards to Europe discovering islands,
the pale ones and the ones like
elephants and those like pearls.

But the trees shall stand never
so high as in his native land!
they hoped, but he found ruins and
aqueducts and fountains, and loved them.

1956

A STEP AWAY FROM THEM

It's my lunch hour, so I go
for a walk among the hum-colored
cabs. First, down the sidewalk
where laborers feed their dirty
glistening torsos sandwiches
and Coca-Cola, with yellow helmets
on. They protect them from falling
bricks, I guess. Then onto the
avenue where skirts are flipping
above heels and blow up over
grates. The sun is hot, but the
cabs stir up the air. I look
at bargains in wristwatches. There
are cats playing in sawdust.
                              On
to Times Square, where the sign
blows smoke over my head, and higher
the waterfall pours lightly. A
Negro stands in a doorway with a
toothpick, languorously agitating.
A blonde chorus girl clicks: he
smiles and rubs his chin. Everything
suddenly honks: it is 12:40 of
a Thursday.
               Neon in daylight is a
great pleasure, as Edwin Denby would
write, as are light bulbs in daylight.
I stop for a cheeseburger at JULIET'S
CORNER. Giulietta Masina, wife of
Federico Fellini, *è bell' attrice.*
And chocolate malted. A lady in
foxes on such a day puts her poodle
in a cab.
          There are several Puerto
Ricans on the avenue today, which
makes it beautiful and warm. First
Bunny died, then John Latouche,

then Jackson Pollock. But is the
earth as full as life was full, of them?
And one has eaten and one walks,
past the magazines with nudes
and the posters for BULLFIGHT and
the Manhattan Storage Warehouse,
which they'll soon tear down. I
used to think they had the Armory
Show there.
          A glass of papaya juice
and back to work. My heart is in my
pocket, it is Poems by Pierre Reverdy.

1956

DIGRESSION ON *NUMBER I, 1948*

I am ill today but I am not
too ill. I am not ill at all.
It is a perfect day, warm
for winter, cold for fall.

A fine day for seeing. I see
ceramics, during lunch hour, by
Miró, and I see the sea by Léger;
light, complicated Metzingers
and a rude awakening by Brauner,
a little table by Picasso, pink.

I am tired today but I am not
too tired. I am not tired at all.
There is the Pollock, white, harm
will not fall, his perfect hand

and the many short voyages. They'll
never fence the silver range.
Stars are out and there is sea
enough beneath the glistening earth
to bear me toward the future
which is not so dark. I see.

1956

[IT SEEMS FAR AWAY AND GENTLE NOW]

It seems far away and gentle now
the morning miseries of childhood
and its raining calms over the schools

Alterable noons of loitering
beside puddles watching leaves swim
and reflected dreams of blue travels

To be always in vigilance away
from the bully who broke my nose
and so I had to break his wristwatch

A surprising violence in the sky
inspired me to my first public act
nubile and pretentious but growing pure

as the whitecaps are the wind's
but a surface agitation of the waters
means a rampart on the ocean floor is falling

And will soon be open to the tender
governing tides of a reigning will
while alterable noon assumes its virtue

1956

WHY I AM NOT A PAINTER

I am not a painter, I am a poet.
Why? I think I would rather be
a painter, but I am not. Well,

for instance, Mike Goldberg
is starting a painting. I drop in.
"Sit down and have a drink" he
says. I drink; we drink. I look
up. "You have SARDINES in it."
"Yes, it needed something there."
"Oh." I go and the days go by
and I drop in again. The painting
is going on, and I go, and the days
go by. I drop in. The painting is
finished. "Where's SARDINES?"
All that's left is just
letters, "It was too much," Mike says.

But me? One day I am thinking of
a color: orange. I write a line
about orange. Pretty soon it is a
whole page of words, not lines.
Then another page. There should be
so much more, not of orange, of
words, of how terrible orange is
and life. Days go by. It is even in
prose, I am a real poet. My poem
is finished and I haven't mentioned
orange yet. It's twelve poems, I call
it ORANGES. And one day in a gallery
I see Mike's painting, called SARDINES.

1956

POEM READ AT JOAN MITCHELL'S

At last you are tired of being single
the effort to be new does not upset you nor the effort to be other
you are not tired of life together

city noises are louder because you are together
being together you arc louder than calling separately across a telephone one to the other
and there is no noise like the rare silence when you both sleep
even country noises—a dog bays at the moon, but when it loves the
        moon it bows, and the hitherto frowning moon fawns and slips

Only you in New York are not boring tonight
it is most modern to affirm some one
(we don't really love ideas, do we?)
and Joan was surprising you with a party for which I was the decoy
but you were surprising us by getting married and going away
so I am here reading poetry anyway
and no one will be bored tonight by me because you're here

Yesterday I felt very tired from being at the FIVE SPOT
and today I felt very tired from going to bed early and reading ULYSSES
but tonight I feel energetic because I'm sort of the bugle,
like waking people up, of your peculiar desire to get married

It's so
original, hydrogenic, anthropomorphic, fiscal, post-anti-esthetic,
        bland, unpicturesque and WilliamCarlosWilliamsian!
it's definitely not 19th Century, it's not even Partisan Review, it's
        new, it must be vanguard!

Tonight you probably walked over here from Bethune Street
down Greenwich Avenue with its sneaky little bars and the Women's Detention House,
across 8th Street, by the acres of books and pillows and shoes and
        illuminating lampshades,
past Cooper Union where we heard the piece by Mortie Feldman with "The
        Stars and Stripes Forever" in it
and the Sagamore's terrific "coffee and, Andy," meaning "with a cheese
        Danish"—

did you spit on your index fingers and rub the CEDAR's neon circle for
          luck?
did you give a kind thought, hurrying, to Alger Hiss?

It's the day before February 17th
it is not snowing yet but it is dark and may snow yet
dreary February of the exhaustion from parties and the exceptional de-
          sire for spring which the ballet alone, by extending its run,
          has made bearable, dear New York City Ballet company, you are
          quite a bit like a wedding yourself!
and the only signs of spring are Maria Tallchief's rhinestones and a
          perky little dog barking in a bar, here and there eyes which
          suddenly light up with blue, like a ripple subsiding under a
          lily pad, or with brown, like a freshly plowed field we vow
          we'll drive out and look at when a certain Sunday comes in May—
and these eyes are undoubtedly Jane's and Joe's because they are ad-
          vancing into spring before us and tomorrow is Sunday

This poem goes on too long because our friendship has been long, long
          for this life and these times, long as art is long and un-
          interruptable,
and I would make it as long as I hope our friendship lasts if I could
          make poems that long

I hope there will be more
more drives to Bear Mountain and searches for hamburgers, more evenings
          avoiding the latest Japanese movie and watching Helen Vinson
          and Warner Baxter in *Vogues of 1938* instead, more discussions
          in lobbies of the respective greatnesses of Diana Adams and
          Allegra Kent,
more sunburns and more half-mile swims in which Joe beats me as Jane
          watches, lotion-covered and sleepy, more arguments over
          Faulkner's inferiority to Tolstoy while sand gets into my
          bathing trunks
let's advance and change everything, but leave these little oases in
          case the heart gets thirsty en route
and I should probably propose myself as a godfather if you have any

children, since I will probably earn more money some day
accidentally, and could teach him or her how to swim
and now there is a Glazunov symphony on the radio and I think of our
friends who are not here, of John and the nuptial quality
of his verses (he is always marrying the whole world) and
Janice and Kenneth, smiling and laughing, respectively (they
are probably laughing at the Leaning Tower right now)
but we are all here and have their proxy
if Kenneth were writing this he would point out how art has changed
women and women have changed art and men, but men haven't
changed women much
but ideas are obscure and nothing should be obscure tonight
you will live half the year in a house by the sea and half the year in
a house in our arms
we peer into the future and see you happy and hope it is a sign that we
will be happy too, something to cling to, happiness
the least and best of human attainments

1957

JOHN BUTTON BIRTHDAY

Sentiments are nice, "The Lonely Crowd,"
a rift in the clouds appears above the purple,
you find a birthday greeting card with violets
which says "a perfect friend" and means
"I love you" but the customer is forced to be
shy. It says less, as all things must.

                                             But
grease sticks to the red ribs shaped like a
sea shell, grease, light and rosy that smells of
sandalwood: it's memory! I remember JA
staggering over to me in the San Remo and murmuring
"I've met someone MARVELLOUS!" That's friendship
for you, and the sentiment of introduction.

And now that I have finished dinner I can continue.

What is it that attracts one to one? Mystery?
I think of you in Paris with a red beard, a
theological student; in London talking to a friend
who lunched with Dowager Queen Mary and offered
her his last cigarette; in Los Angeles shopping
at the Supermarket; on Mount Shasta, looking . . .
above all on Mount Shasta in your unknown youth
and photograph.
                           And then the way you straighten
people out. How ambitious you are! And that you're
a painter is a great satisfaction, too. You know how
I feel about painters. I sometimes think poetry
only describes.
                          Now I have taken down the underwear
I washed last night from the various light fixtures
and can proceed.
                         And the lift of our experiences
together, which seem to me legendary. The long subways
to our old neighborhood the near East 49th and 53rd,
and before them the laughing in bars till we cried,

and the crying in movies till we laughed, the tenting
tonight on the old camp grounds! How beautiful it is
to visit someone for instant coffee! and you visiting
Cambridge, Massachusetts, talking for two weeks worth
in hours, and watching Maria Tallchief in the Public
Gardens while the swan-boats slumbered. And now,
not that I'm interrupting again, I mean your now,
you are 82 and I am 03. And in 1984 I trust we'll still
be high together. I'll say "Let's go to a bar"
and you'll say "Let's go to a movie" and we'll go to both;
like two old Chinese drunkards arguing about their
favorite mountain and the million reasons for them both.

1957

ANXIETY

I'm having a real day of it.
                              There was
something I had to do. But what?
There are no alternatives, just
the one something.
                              I have a drink,
it doesn't help—far from it!
                                        I
feel worse. I can't remember how
I felt, so perhaps I feel better.
No. Just a little darker.
                              If I could
get really dark, richly dark, like
being drunk, that's the best that's
open as a field. Not the best,

but the best except for the impossible
pure light, to be as if above a vast
prairie, rushing and pausing over
the tiny golden heads in deep grass. ·

1957

LOUISE

Sometimes I think I see a tiny figure
sidling through the Bush. Yes, there
at the edge of the forest, blinking in
new light. It must have wandered up
from Down Under. I believe it's Maldoror!

And now, having decided, it starts
the weary trek across the rolling plain,
pausing occasionally beneath a shade
or on the gently sloping rise. It rests,
too, on the crater of a long defunct
volcano, lying down for a time in its
wrinkles.
      Then onward again, through
the valley bounded by Twin Peaks, pink
in the sunlight, with the scattered
forests coming down right to the edge
of the pass.
      Disappearing for almost
a day, or is it night? the toiling figure
suddenly finds itself in a clearing.
(Suddenly to me!) Then there is an upheaval
rather like an earthquake. It clings
for dear life to the nearest overhanging
branch.
      There it is stranded in the blue
gaze. And the gaze is astonished, eye
to eye: a speck, and a vastness staring
back at it. Why it's Louise! Hi, Louise.

1957

FAILURES OF SPRING

I'm getting rather Lorcaesque lately
and I don't like it.
         Better if my poetry were,
instead of my lives. So many aspects of a star,

the Rudolph Valentino of sentimental reaction
to dives and crumby ex-jazz-hangouts.
                  I
put on my sheik's outfit and sit down
at the pianola,
        like when I first discovered
aspirin.
       And I shall never make my LORCAESCAS
into an opera. I don't write opera.
             So hot,
so hot the night my world
          is trying to send up
        its observation satellite.

1957

TWO DREAMS OF WAKING

1

I stumble over furniture, I fall into a gloomy hammock
on a rainy day in Cape Cod years ago. It is a black hardoy chair.
I reach the kitchen and Joe is making coffee in the dark.
I can't face him, because we both have to go to work
and we hate work. I look into the corner of a shelf. "Work
interrupts life," he is muttering as he splashes in the sink.
I can't remember what he's doing, just that his back
was pale gold. I don't look at it. Two white mice, big,
are running through the hole in the sleeve of my raspberry sweater.
They seem to be harming it. I shout at them. I appeal, "it's already wearing out,"
to Joe. He looks at me coldly. "Leave them alone. They're
playing. They have to live, too, don't they?"
I have a hangover, and he hates me for it, and we start for work,

2

I stagger out of bed
and there are flashes
of light. I stand naked
in a certain posture.
It is Larry welding a
figure and he says, "I'm
glad you're developing breasts.
I want you to pose for
the legs of this thing."
I look and I am the same.
"It's all the same," he
says, "I just looked at Jane's
breasts. She's menstruating
and the veins beneath the
hair on your chest are
just like those on her breasts."
I get scared. "I'm not
menstruating, I'm peeing."
I am. There is a chamber pot
forming a triangle with
my feet and the arc of my
pee slopes like a thigh.

It reminds me of a nude in
a painting I can't remember.
I get scared again. "You think,"
Larry says, "that you're safe
because you have a penis. So
do I, but we're both wrong."
He starts banging on the steel
again and the sound puts me
to sleep standing up. I feel
that years are going by
and I can't talk to them or anything.

1957

ODE TO JOY

We shall have everything we want and there'll be no more dying
    on the pretty plains or in the supper clubs
for our symbol we'll acknowledge vulgar materialistic laughter
    over an insatiable sexual appetite
and the streets will be filled with racing forms
and the photographs of murderers and narcissists and movie stars
    will swell from the walls and books alive in steaming rooms
    to press against our burning flesh not once but interminably
as water flows down hill into the full-lipped basin
and the adder dives for the ultimate ostrich egg
and the feather cushion preens beneath a reclining monolith
    that's sweating with post-exertion visibility and sweetness
    near the grave of love

                          No more dying

We shall see the grave of love as a lovely sight and temporary
    near the elm that spells the lovers' names in roots
and there'll be no more music but the ears in lips and no more wit
    but tongues in ears and no more drums but ears to thighs
as evening signals nudities unknown to ancestors' imaginations
and the imagination itself will stagger like a tired paramour of ivory
    under the sculptural necessities of lust that never falters
    like a six-mile runner from Sweden or Liberia covered with gold
as lava flows up and over the far-down somnolent city's abdication
and the hermit always wanting to be lone is lone at last
and the weight of external heat crushes the heat-hating Puritan
    whose self-defeating vice becomes a proper sepulchre at last
    that love may live

Buildings will go up into the dizzy air as love itself goes in
    and up the reeling life that it has chosen for once or all
while in the sky a feeling of intemperate fondness will excite the birds
    to swoop and veer like flies crawling across absorbèd limbs
that weep a pearly perspiration on the sheets of brief attention
and the hairs dry out that summon anxious declaration of the organs
    as they rise like buildings to the needs of temporary neighbors
    pouring hunger through the heart to feed desire in intravenous ways

like the ways of gods with humans in the innocent combination of light
and flesh or as the legends ride their heroes through the dark to found
great cities where all life is possible to maintain as long as time
   which wants us to remain for cocktails in a bar and after dinner
   lets us live with it
                       No more dying

1957

ODE TO WILLEM DE KOONING

Beyond the sunrise
where the black begins

                           an enormous city
                           is sending up its shutters

and just before the last lapse of nerve which I am already sorry for,
that friends describe as "just this once" in a temporary hell, I hope

I try to seize upon greatness
which is available to me

                           through generosity and
                           lavishness of spirit, yours

not to be inimitably weak
and picturesque, my self

                           but to be standing clearly
                           alone in the orange wind

while our days tumble and rant through Gotham and the Easter narrows
and I have not the courage to convict myself of cowardice or care

for now a long history slinks over the sill, or patent absurdities
and the fathomless miseries of a small person upset by personality

and I look to the flags
in your eyes as they go up

                           on the enormous walls
                           as the brave must always ascend

into the air, always the musts
like banderillas dangling

and jingling jewellike amidst the red drops on the shoulders of men
who lead us not forward or backward, but on as we must go on

                           out into the mesmerized world
                           of inanimate voices like traffic

noises, hewing a clearing
in the crowded abyss of the West

2

Stars of all passing sights,
language, thought and reality,
"I am assuming that one knows
what it is to be ashamed"
and that the light we seek
is broad and pure, not winking
and that the evil inside us
now and then strolls into a field
and sits down like a forgotten rock
while we walk on to a horizon
line that's beautifully keen,
precarious and doesn't sag
beneath our variable weight

In this dawn as in the first
it's the Homeric rose, its scent
that leads us up the rocky path
into the pass where death
can disappear or where the face
of future senses may appear
in a white night that opens
after the embattled hours of day

And the wind tears up the rose
fountains of prehistoric light
falling upon the blinded heroes
who did not see enough or were not
mad enough or felt too little
when the blood began to pour down
the rocky slopes into pink seas

3

Dawn must always recur
                    to blot out stars and the terrible systems
of belief
          Dawn, which dries out the web so the wind can blow it,
                    spider and all, away

Dawn,
       erasing blindness from an eye inflamed,
                      reaching for its
morning cigarette in Promethean inflection
                  after the blames
and desperate conclusions of the dark
                where messages were intercepted
by an ignorant horde of thoughts
          and all simplicities perished in desire

A bus crashes into a milk truck
               and the girl goes skating up the avenue
with streaming hair
        roaring through fluttering newspapers
and their Athenian contradictions
          for democracy is joined
with stunning collapsible savages, all natural and relaxed and free

as the day zooms into space and only darkness lights our lives,
with few flags flaming, imperishable courage and the gentle will
which is the individual dawn of genius rising from its bed

"maybe they're wounds, but maybe they are rubies"
              each painful as a sun

                1957

POEM

I live above a dyke bar and I'm happy.
The police car is always near the door
                              in case they cry
or the key doesn't work in the lock. But
            he can't open it either. So we go to Joan's
and sleep over
                  Bridget and Joe and I.

I meet Mike for a beer in the Cedar as
the wind flops up the Place, pushing the leaves
against the streetlights. And Norman tells about

the geste,
            with the individual significance of a hardon
like humanity.
                  We go to Irma's for Bloody Marys,

and then it's dark.
We played with her cat and it fell asleep. We
seem very mild. It's humid out. (Are they spelled "dikes"?)
People say they are Bacchantes, but if they are

we must be the survivors of Thermopylae.

                                            1957

ODE TO MICHAEL GOLDBERG ('S BIRTH AND OTHER BIRTHS)

I don't remember anything of then, down there around the magnolias
       where I was no more comfortable than I've been since
       though aware of a certain neutrality called satisfaction
       sometimes

and there's never been an opportunity to think of it as an idyll
as if everyone'd been singing around me, or around a tulip tree

a faint stirring of that singing seems to come to me in heavy traffic
but I can't be sure that's it, it may be some more recent singing
from hours of dusk in bushes playing tag, being called in, walking
       up onto the porch crying bitterly because it wasn't a veranda
"smell that honeysuckle?" or a door you can see through terribly clearly,
          even the mosquitoes saw through it
suffocating netting
or more often being put into a brown velvet suit and kicked around
perhaps that was my last real cry for myself
in a forest you think of birds, in traffic you think of tires,
       where are you?
in Baltimore you think of hats and shoes, like Daddy did

            I hardly ever think of June 27, 1926
            when I came moaning into my mother's world
            and tried to make it mine immediately
            by screaming, sucking, urinating
            and carrying on generally
            it was quite a day

I wasn't proud of my penis yet, how did I know how to act? it was 1936
"no excuses, now"

   Yellow morning
          silent, wet
               blackness under the trees over stone walls
hay, smelling faintly of semen
              a few sheltered flowers nodding and smiling

at the clattering cutter-bar
                        of the mower ridden by Jimmy Whitney
"I'd like to put my rolling-pin to her"   his brother Bailey
leaning on his pitchfork, watching
                            "you shove it in and nine months later
it comes out a kid"
                    Ha ha   where those flowers would dry out
and never again be seen
                    except as cow-flaps, hushed noon drinking cold
water in the dusty field   "their curly throats"   big milk cans

        full of cold spring water, sandy hair, black hair

        I went to my first movie
        and the hero got his legs
        cut off by a steam engine
        in a freightyard, in my second

        Karen Morley got shot
        in the back by an arrow
        I think she was an heiress
        it came through her bathroom door

        there was nobody there
        there never was anybody
        there at any time
        in sweet-smelling summer

I'd like to stay
            in this field forever
                            and think of nothing
but these sounds,
            these smells and the tickling grasses
                            "up your ass, Sport"

        Up on the mountainous hill
        behind the confusing house

where I lived, I went each
day after school and some nights
with my various dogs, the
terrier that bit people, Arno
the shepherd (who used to
be wild but had stopped), the
wire-haired that took fits
and finally the boring gentle
cocker, spotted brown and white,
   named Freckles   there,

the wind sounded exactly like
Stravinsky
              I first recognized art
as wildness, and it seemed right,
              I mean rite, to me

climbing the water tower I'd
look out for hours in wind
and the world seemed rounder
and fiercer and I was happier
because I wasn't scared of falling off

nor off the horses, the horses!
to hell with the horses, bay and black

It's odd to have secrets at an early age, trysts
whose thoughtfulness and sweetness are those of a very aggressive person
        carried beneath your shirt like an amulet against your sire
            what one must do is done in a red twilight
                    on colossally old and dirty furniture with knobs,
            and on Sunday afternoons you meet in a high place
                watching the Sunday drivers and the symphonic sadness
            stopped, a man in a convertible put his hand up a girl's skirt
        and again the twitching odor of hay, like a minor irritation
    that gives you a hardon, and again the roundness of horse noises

"Je suis las de vivre au pays natal"
　　　but unhappiness, like Mercury, transfixed me
　　there, un repaire de vipères
　　　　and had I known the strength and durability
of those invisible bonds I would have leaped from rafters onto prongs
then
　　　　and been carried shining and intact
　　　　to the Indian Cemetery near the lake

　　　　　　　　　　　but there is a glistening
　　　　　　　　　　　blackness in the center
　　　　　　　　　　　if you seek it

here . . .　　it's capable of bursting
　　　　　into flame or merely
　　　　　gleaming profoundly in

　　　　　　　　　　　the platinum setting
　　　　　　　　　　　of your ornamental
　　　　　　　　　　　human ties and hates

hanging between breasts
　　　　　　　　or, crosslike, on a chest of hairs
the center of myself is never silent
　　　　　　　　　　the wind soars, keening overhead
and the vestments of unnatural safety
　　　　　　　　　　part to reveal a foreign land
toward whom I have been selected to bear
　　　　　　　　　　　the gift of fire
　　　　　　　　the temporary place of light, the land of air

down where a flame illumines gravity and means warmth and insight,
　　　where air is flesh, where speed is darkness
and
　　　things can suddenly be reached, held, dropped and known

where a not totally imaginary ascent can begin all over again in tears

　　　A couple of specifically anguished days
　　　make me now distrust sorrow, simple sorrow
　　　especially, like sorrow over death

it makes you wonder who you are to be sorrowful
over death, death belonging to another
and suddenly inhabited by you without permission

you moved in impulsively and took it up
declaring your Squatters' Rights in howls
or screaming with rage, like a parvenu in a Chinese laundry

disbelieving your own feelings is the worst
and you suspect that you are jealous of this death

    YIPPEE! I'm glad I'm alive
                      "I'm glad you're alive
  too, baby, because I want to fuck you"
                         you are pink
  and despicable in the warm breeze drifting in the window
and the rent
        is due, in honor of which you have borrowed $34.96 from Joe
and it's all over but the smoldering hatred of pleasure
  a gorgeous purple like somebody's favorite tie
    "Shit, that means you're getting kind of ascetic, doesn't it?"

      So I left, the stars were shining
      like the lights around a swimming pool

      you've seen a lot of anemones, too
      haven't you, Old Paint? through the
      Painted Desert to the orange covered
      slopes where a big hill was moving in
      on L A and other stars were strolling
      in shorts down palm-stacked horse-walks
      and I stared with my strained SP stare
      wearing a gun
                the doubts
   of a life devoted to leaving rumors of love for new
from does she love me to do I love him,

                                        sempiternal farewell to hearths
and the gods who don't live there

                    in New Guinea a Sunday morning figure
                    reclining outside his hut in Lamourish languor
                    and an atabrine-dyed hat like a sick sun
                    over his ebony land on your way to breakfast

                    he has had his balls sewed into his mouth
                    by the natives who bleach their hair in urine
                    and their will; a basketball game and a concert
                    later if you live to write, it's not all advancing
                    towards you, he had a killing desire for their women

        but more killing still the absence of desire, which in religion
                                        used to be called hope,
I don't just mean the lack of a hardon, which may be sincerity
                        or the last-minute victory of the proud spirit over flesh,
        no: a tangerinelike sullenness in the face of sunrise
                        or a dark sinking in the wind on the forecastle
        when someone you love hits your head and says "I'd sail with you any
                                        where, war or no war"
    who was about
                    to die a tough blond death
                                        like a slender blighted palm
    in the hurricane's curious hail
                            and the maelstrom of bulldozers
                    and metal sinkings,
                                        churning the earth
    even under the fathomless deaths
                            below, beneath
                                        where the one special
                    went to be hidden, never to disappear
                    not spatial in that way

        Take me, I felt, into the future fear of saffron pleasures
crazy strangeness and steam

of seeing a (pearl) white whale, steam of
being high in the sky
opening fire on Corsairs,
kept moving in berths
where I trade someone *The Counterfeiters* (I thought it was about personal
freedom then!) for a pint of whiskey,
banana brandy in Manila, spidery
steps trailing down onto the rocks of the harbor
and up in the black fir, the
pyramidal whiteness, Genji on the Ginza,
a lavender-kimono-sized
loneliness,
and drifting into my ears off Sendai in the snow Carl
T. Fischer's *Recollections of an Indian Boy*
this tiny overdecorated
rock garden bringing obviously heart-shaped
the Great Plains, as is
my way to be obvious as eight o'clock in the dining car
of the
20th Century Limited (express)
and its noisy blast passing buttes to be
Atchison-Topeka-Santa Fé, Baltimore and Ohio (Cumberland),
leaving
beds in Long Beach for beds in Boston, via C- (D,B,) 47 (6)
pretty girls in textile mills,
drowsing on bales in a warehouse of cotton
listening to soft Southern truck talk
perhaps it is "your miraculous
low roar" on Ulithi as the sailors pee into funnels, ambassadors of
green-beer-interests bigger than Standard Oil in the South
Pacific, where the beaches flower with cat-eyes and ear fungus
warm as we never wanted to be warm, in an ammunition
dump, my foot again crushed (this time by a case of 40 millimeters)
"the
only thing you ever gave New Guinea was your toenail and now
the Australians are taking over"   . . . the pony of war?

to "return" safe who will never feel safe
and loves to ride steaming in the autumn of
centuries of useless aspiration towards artifice
           are you feeling useless, too, Old Paint?
I am really an Indian at heart, knowing it is all
all over but my own ceaseless going, never
to be just a hill of dreams and flint for someone later
but a hull laved by the brilliant Celebes response,
empty of treasure to the explorers who sailed me not

King Philip's trail,
                lachrymose highway of infantile regrets and cayuse
meannesses,
                Mendelssohn driving me mad in Carnegie Hall like greed
grasping
           Palisades Park smiling, you pull a pretty ring out of the pineapple
and blow yourself up
                           contented to be a beautiful fan of blood
                           above the earth-empathic earth

           Now suddenly the fierce wind of disease and Venus, as
when a child
                you wonder if you're not a little crazy, laughing
because a horse
                   is standing on your foot
                                   and you're kicking his hock
with your sneaker, which is to him
                                   a love-tap, baring big teeth
laughing . . .
                thrilling activities which confuse
                                       too many, too loud
too often, crowds of intimacies and no distance
                                       the various cries
and rounds
                and we are smiling in our confused way, darkly
in the back alcove

                        of the Five Spot, devouring chicken-in-the-basket
        and arguing,
                        the four of us, about loyalty

                        wonderful stimulation of bitterness
                        to be young and to grow bigger
                        more and more cells, like germs
                        or a political conspiracy

                        and each reason for love always
                        a certain hostility, mistaken
                        for wisdom
                                        exceptional excitement
                        which is finally simple blindness
                        (but not to be sneezed at!) like
                        a successful American satellite . . .

                        Yes, it does, it would still
                        keep me out of a monastery if
                        I were invited to attend one

                                        from round the window, you can't
                see the street!
                                you let the cold wind course through
        and let the heart pump and gurgle
                                in febrile astonishment,
                                                a cruel world
        to which you've led it by your mind,
                                bicycling no-hands
                                                leaving it gasping
        there, wondering where you are and how to get back
                                                although you'll never let
                        it go

                while somewhere everything's dispersed
        at five o'clock
                        for Martinis a group of professional freshnesses meet

and the air's like a shrub—Rose o'Sharon? the others,

                                                      it's not

a flickering light for us, but the glare of the dark

                                     too much endlessness

stored up, and in store:

                    "the exquisite prayer
                    to be new each day
                    brings to the artist
                    only a certain kneeness"

I am assuming that everything is all right and difficult,

                                       where hordes

           of stars carry the burdens of the gentler animals like our-
           selves with wit and austerity beneath a hazardous settlement
           which we understand because we made

                                   and secretly admire

           because it moves

yes! for always, for it is our way, to pass the teahouse and the ceremony
           by and rather fall sobbing to the floor with joy and freezing
           than to spill the kid upon the table and then thank the blood

           for flowing

                  as it must throughout the miserable, clear and willful

life we love beneath the blue,

                  a fleece of pure intention sailing like

a pinto in a barque of slaves

                  who soon will turn upon their captors

lower anchor, found a city riding there

                      of poverty and sweetness paralleled

           among the races without time,

                       and one alone will speak of being

           born in pain

                and he will be the wings of an extraordinary liberty

                                              1958

ODE (TO JOSEPH LESUEUR) ON THE ARROW THAT FLIETH BY DAY

To humble yourself before a radio on a Sunday
it's amusing, like dying after a party
"click"/and you're dead from fall-out, hang-over
        or something hyphenated

(hello, Western Union? send a Mother's Day message to Russia: SORRY
NOT TO BE WITH YOU ON YOUR DAY LOVE AND KISSES TELL THE CZAR LA GRANDE
JATTE WASN'T DAMAGED IN THE MUSEUM OF MODERN ART FIRE /S/ FRANK)

the unrecapturable nostalgia for nostalgia
for a life I might have hated, thus mourned

but do we really need anything more to be sorry about
wouldn't it be extra, as all pain is extra

(except that I will never feel CONTEST: WIN A DREAM TRIP pertains to
me, somehow   Joe, I wouldn't go, probably)

for God's sake fly the other way
leave me standing alone crumbling in the new sky of the Wide World
without passage, without breath

a spatial representative of emptiness

if Joan says I'm wounded, then I'm wounded
and not like La Pucelle or André Gide
not by moral issues or the intercontinental ballistics missile
        or the Seer of Prague

(you're right to go to Aaron's PIANO FANTASY, but I'm not up to it this
time, too important a piece not to punish me
                and it's raining)

it's more like the death of a nation
henceforth to be called small

although its people could say "Mare nostrum" without fear of hubris
and the air saluted them
                    (air of the stars) ashore or leaning on the prow

                                        1958

ODE ON CAUSALITY

There is the sense of neurotic coherence

you think maybe poetry is too important and you like that

suddenly everyone's supposed to be veined, like marble

it isn't that simple but it's simple enough

the rock is least living of the forms man has fucked

and it isn't pathetic and it's lasting, one towering tree

in the vast smile of bronze and vertiginous grasses

Maude lays down her doll, red wagon and her turtle
takes my hand and comes with us, shows the bronze JACKSON POLLOCK
gazelling on the rock of her demeanor as a child, says running
away hand in hand "he isn't under there, he's out in the woods" beyond

and like that child at your grave make me be distant and imaginative
make my lines thin as ice, then swell like pythons
the color of Aurora when she first brought fire to the Arctic in a sled
a sexual bliss inscribe upon the page of whatever energy I burn for art
and do not watch over my life, but read and read through copper earth

not to fall at all, but disappear or burn! seizing a grave by throat
which is the look of earth, its ambiguity of light and sound
the thickness in a look of lust, the air within the eye
the gasp of a moving hand as maps change and faces become vacant
it's noble to refuse to be added up or divided, finality of kings

                    and there's the ugliness we seek in vain
through life and long for like a mortuarian Baudelaire working for Skouras
inhabiting neighborhoods of Lear! Lear! Lear!
                                        tenement of a single heart

for Old Romance was draping dolors on a scarlet mound, each face
a country of valorous decay, heath-helmet or casque, *mollement, moelleusement*
and all that shining fierce turned green and covered the lays with grass
as later in *The Orange Ballad of Cromwell's Charm Upon the Height "So Green"*
as in the histories of that same time and earlier, when written down at all
sweet scripts to obfuscate the tender subjects of their future lays

to be layed at all! romanticized, elaborated, fucked, sung, put to "rest"
is worse than the mild apprehension of a Buddhist type caught halfway up
the tea-rose trellis with his sickle banging on the Monk's lead window, moon
not our moon
              unless the tea exude a little gas and poisonous fact
to reach the spleen and give it a dreamless twinge that love's love's near

     the bang of alertness, loneliness, position that prehends experience .

not much to be less, not much to be more
                     alive, sick; and dead, dying
like the kiss of love meeting the kiss of hatred
                    "oh you know why"
each in asserting beginning to be more of the opposite
                    what goes up must
come down, what dooms must do, standing still and walking in New York

let us walk in that nearby forest, staring into the growling trees
in which an era of pompous frivolity or two is dangling its knobby knees
and reaching for an audience
              over the pillar of our deaths a cloud
heaves
     pushed, steaming and blasted
              love-propelled and tangled glitteringly
        has earned himself the title *Bird in Flight*

1958

ODE: SALUTE TO THE FRENCH NEGRO POETS

From near the sea, like Whitman my great predecessor, I call
to the spirits of other lands to make fecund my existence

do not spare your wrath upon our shores, that trees may grow
upon the sea, mirror of our total mankind in the weather

one who no longer remembers dancing in the heat of the moon may call
across the shifting sands, trying to live in the terrible western world

here where to love at all's to be a politician, as to love a poem
is pretentious, this may sound tendentious but it's lyrical

which shows what lyricism has been brought to by our fabled times
where cowards are shibboleths and one specific love's traduced

by shame for what you love more generally and never would avoid
where reticence is paid for by a poet in his blood or ceasing to be

blood! blood that we have mountains in our veins to stand off jackals
in the pillaging of our desires and allegiances, Aimé Césaire

for if there is fortuity it's in the love we bear each other's differences
in race which is the poetic ground on which we rear our smiles

standing in the sun of marshes as we wade slowly toward the culmination
of a gift which is categorically the most difficult relationship

and should be sought as such because it is our nature, nothing
inspires us but the love we want upon the frozen face of earth

and utter disparagement turns into praise as generations read the message
of our hearts in adolescent closets who once shot at us in doorways

or kept us from living freely because they were too young then to know
what they would ultimately need from a barren and heart-sore life

the beauty of America, neither cool jazz nor devoured Egyptian heroes, lies in
lives in the darkness I inhabit in the midst of sterile millions

the only truth is face to face, the poem whose words become your mouth
and dying in black and white we fight for what we love, not are

1958

A TRUE ACCOUNT OF TALKING
TO THE SUN AT FIRE ISLAND

The Sun woke me this morning loud
and clear, saying "Hey! I've been
trying to wake you up for fifteen
minutes. Don't be so rude, you are
only the second poet I've ever chosen
to speak to personally

                    so why
aren't you more attentive? If I could
burn you through the window I would
to wake you up. I can't hang around
here all day."

              "Sorry, Sun, I stayed
up late last night talking to Hal."

"When I woke up Mayakovsky he was
a lot more prompt" the Sun said
petulantly. "Most people are up
already waiting to see if I'm going
to put in an appearance."

                    I tried
to apologize "I missed you yesterday."
"That's better" he said. "I didn't
know you'd come out." "You may be
wondering why I've come so close?"
"Yes" I said beginning to feel hot
wondering if maybe he wasn't burning me
anyway.

           "Frankly I wanted to tell you
I like your poetry. I see a lot
on my rounds and you're okay. You may
not be the greatest thing on earth, but
you're different. Now, I've heard some
say you're crazy, they being excessively
calm themselves to my mind, and other

crazy poets think that you're a boring
reactionary. Not me.

                     Just keep on
like I do and pay no attention. You'll
find that people always will complain
about the atmosphere, either too hot
or too cold too bright or too dark, days
too short or too long.

                        If you don't appear
at all one day they think you're lazy
or dead. Just keep right on, I like it.

And don't worry about your lineage
poetic or natural. The Sun shines on
the jungle, you know, on the tundra
the sea, the ghetto. Wherever you were
I knew it and saw you moving. I was waiting
for you to get to work.

                       And now that you
are making your own days, so to speak,
even if no one reads you but me
you won't be depressed. Not
everyone can look up, even at me. It
hurts their eyes."

                  "Oh Sun, I'm so grateful to you!"

"Thanks and remember I'm watching. It's
easier for me to speak to you out
here. I don't have to slide down
between buildings to get your ear.
I know you love Manhattan, but
you ought to look up more often.

                          And
always embrace things, people earth

sky stars, as I do, freely and with
the appropriate sense of space. That
is your inclination, known in the heavens
and you should follow it to hell, if
necessary, which I doubt.
                              Maybe we'll
speak again in Africa, of which I too
am specially fond. Go back to sleep now
Frank, and I may leave a tiny poem
in that brain of yours as my farewell."

"Sun, don't go!" I was awake
at last. "No, go I must, they're calling
me."
        "Who are they?"
                              Rising he said "Some
day you'll know. They're calling to you
too." Darkly he rose, and then I slept.

1958

FOU-RIRE

It really is amusing
that for all the centuries of mankind
the problem has been how
to kill enough people
and now
it is how
not to kill them all

1958

TO GOTTFRIED BENN

Poetry is not instruments
that work at times
then walk out on you
laugh at you old
get drunk on you young
poetry's part of your self

like the passion of a nation
at war it moves quickly
provoked to defense or aggression
unreasoning power
an instinct for self-declaration

like nations its faults are absorbed
in the heat of sides and angles
combatting the void of rounds
a solid of imperfect placement
nations get worse and worse

but not wrongly revealed
in the universal light of tragedy

1958

HEROIC SCULPTURE

We join the animals
not when we fuck
            or shit
not when tear falls

but when
            staring into light
            we think

1958

THE "UNFINISHED"

In memory of Bunny Lang

As happiness takes off the tie it borrowed from me
and gets into bed and pretends to be asleep-and-awake
or pulls an orange poncho over its blonde Jay-Thorped curls
and goes off to cocktails without telling me why
it's so depressing,
            so I will be as unhappy as I damn well
please and not make too much of it because I am
really here and not in a novel or anything or a jet plane
as I've often gone away on a ladder, a taxi or a jet plane

      everybody thinks if you go, you go up
but I'm not so sure about that because the fault of my generation
is that nobody wants to make a big *histoire* about anything
and I'm just like everybody else, if an earthquake comes
laughingly along and gulps down the whole of Madrid
including the Manzanares River and for dessert all the royal tombs
in the Escorial I'd only get kind of hysterical about one person
no Voltaire me
          and isn't it funny how beautiful Sibelius sounds
if you haven't found him for a long time? because if we didn't all
hang onto a little self-conscious bitterness and call it intelligence
and admire it as technique we would all be perfectly truthful
and fall into the vat of longing and suffocate in its suet
except for the two Gregorys
              Lafayette who was so pointlessly handsome
and innocently blond that he cheerfully died
                and Corso
too lustrously dark and precise, he would be excavated and declared
a black diamond and hung round a slender bending neck
in the 26th Century when the Court of the Bourbons is reinstated
and heaven comes to resemble more closely a late Goya

      this isn't bitterness, it's merely a tremor of the earth
I'm impersonating some wretch weeping over a 1956 date book and of course
I pull myself together and then I wipe my eyes and see that it's my own
           (date book, that is)
and everything becomes history: when Lennie Bernstein conducted it

on TV last week he called it my Symphony Number One, my "Unfinished"
that sort of thing can give you a terrible feeling that you've
                    accomplished something

meanwhile, back at the Paris branch of contemporary depression, I
am dropping through the famous blueness like a pearl diver, I am
looking for Gregory who lives on Heart-Bed Street and I sit with Ashbery
in the Flore because of his poem about himself in a flower-bed
and we look for Gregory in the Deux Magots because I want to cry with him
about a dear dead friend, it's always about dying, never about death
I sometimes think it's the only reason that any of us love each other
it is raining, Ashes helps me finish my gall and seltzer, and we go

            the casual reader will not, I am sure, be averse to a short
            digression in this splendid narrative by which the nature
            of the narrator can be more or less revealed and all sorts
            of things subsequently become clearer if not clear: picture
            a person who one day in a fit of idleness decides to make
            a pomander like the one that granny used to have around the
            house in old New England and so he takes an orange and sticks
            a lot of cloves in it and then he looks at it and realizes
            that he's killed the orange, his favorite which came from
            the Malay Archipelago and was even loved in Ancient China,
            and he quickly pulls out all the cloves, but it's too
            late! Orange is lying bleeding in my hand! and I
            suddenly think of the moon, hanging quietly up there
            ever since the time of Keats, and now they're shoot-
            ing all those funny-looking things at her, that's
            what you get, baby (end of digression)

and back in New York Gregory is back in New York and we are still missing
each other in the Cedar and in hotel lobbies where Salvador Dali is
supposed to be asleep and at Anne Truxell's famous giggling parties
until one fine day (vedremo) we meet over a duck dinner, good god
I just remembered what he stuffed it with, you guessed it: oranges!
and perhaps, too, he is the true narrator of this story, Gregory

no, I must be, because he's in Chicago, and after all those months
including Madrid where it turns out there wasn't any earthquake
and also the TV broadcast was cancelled because Bernstein had a sore
thumb, I'm not depressed any more, because Gregory has had the same
experience with oranges, and is alive

     where all memories grow into childhood
     and mingled sound and silence drifts up to the rooftop
     where a bare-legged boy stares into the future
     takes up the knives of his wounds to catch the light
     foreseeing his epic triumph in the style of Cecil B. De Mille
     when one day the Via del Corso is named after him
     the principal street of Rome
     which is better than the Nobel Prize
     better than Albert Schweitzer, Pablo Casals and Helen Keller
     PUT TO GETHER

1959

THE DAY LADY DIED

It is 12:20 in New York a Friday
three days after Bastille day, yes
it is 1959 and I go get a shoeshine
because I will get off the 4:19 in Easthampton
at 7:15 and then go straight to dinner
and I don't know the people who will feed me

I walk up the muggy street beginning to sun
and have a hamburger and a malted and buy
an ugly NEW WORLD WRITING to see what the poets
in Ghana are doing these days
                              I go on to the bank
and Miss Stillwagon (first name Linda I once heard)
doesn't even look up my balance for once in her life
and in the GOLDEN GRIFFIN I get a little Verlaine
for Patsy with drawings by Bonnard although I do
think of Hesiod, trans. Richmond Lattimore or
Brendan Behan's new play or *Le Balcon* or *Les Nègres*
of Genet, but I don't, I stick with Verlaine
after practically going to sleep with quandariness

and for Mike I just stroll into the PARK LANE
Liquor Store and ask for a bottle of Strega and
then I go back where I came from to 6th Avenue
and the tobacconist in the Ziegfeld Theatre and
casually ask for a carton of Gauloises and a carton
of Picayunes, and a NEW YORK POST with her face on it

and I am sweating a lot by now and thinking of
leaning on the john door in the 5 SPOT
while she whispered a song along the keyboard
to Mal Waldron and everyone and I stopped breathing

1959

155

RHAPSODY

515 Madison Avenue
door to heaven? portal
stopped realities and eternal licentiousness
or at least the jungle of impossible eagerness
your marble is bronze and your lianas elevator cables
swinging from the myth of ascending
I would join
or declining the challenge of racial attractions
they zing on (into the lynch, dear friends)
while everywhere love is breathing draftily
like a doorway linking 53rd with 54th
the east-bound with the west-bound traffic by 8,000,000s
o midtown tunnels and the tunnels, too, of Holland

where is the summit where all aims are clear
the pin-point light upon a fear of lust
as agony's needlework grows up around the unicorn
and fences him for milk- and yoghurt-work
when I see Gianni I know he's thinking of John Ericson
playing the Rachmaninoff 2nd or Elizabeth Taylor
taking sleeping-pills and Jane thinks of Manderley
and Irkutsk while I cough lightly in the smog of desire
and my eyes water achingly imitating the true blue

a sight of Manahatta in the towering needle
multi-faceted insight of the fly in the stringless labyrinth
Canada plans a higher place than the Empire State Building
I am getting into a cab at 9th Street and 1st Avenue
and the Negro driver tells me about a $120 apartment
"where you can't walk across the floor after 10 at night
not even to pee, cause it keeps them awake downstairs"
no, I don't like that "well, I didn't take it"
perfect in the hot humid morning on my way to work
a little supper-club conversation for the mill of the gods

you were there always and you know all about these things
as indifferent as an encyclopedia with your calm brown eyes

it isn't enough to smile when you run the gauntlet
you've got to spit like Niagara Falls on everybody or
Victoria Falls or at least the beautiful urban fountains of Madrid
as the Niger joins the Gulf of Guinea near the Menemsha Bar
that is what you learn in the early morning passing Madison Avenue
where you've never spent any time and stores eat up light

I have always wanted to be near it
though the day is long (and I don't mean Madison Avenue)
lying in a hammock on St. Mark's Place sorting my poems
in the rancid nourishment of this mountainous island
they are coming and we holy ones must go
is Tibet historically a part of China? as I historically
belong to the enormous bliss of American death

1959

SONG

Is it dirty
does it look dirty
that's what you think of in the city

does it just seem dirty
that's what you think of in the city
you don't refuse to breathe do you

someone comes along with a very bad character
he seems attractive. is he really. yes. very
he's attractive as his character is bad. is it. yes

that's what you think of in the city
run your finger along your no-moss mind
that's not a thought that's soot

and you take a lot of dirt off someone
is the character less bad. no. it improves constantly
you don't refuse to breathe do you

1959

ADIEU TO NORMAN,
BON JOUR TO JOAN AND JEAN-PAUL

It is 12:10 in New York and I am wondering
if I will finish this in time to meet Norman for lunch
ah lunch! I think I am going crazy
what with my terrible hangover and the weekend coming up
at excitement-prone Kenneth Koch's
I wish I were staying in town and working on my poems
at Joan's studio for a new book by Grove Press
which they will probably not print
but it is good to be several floors up in the dead of night
wondering whether you are any good or not
and the only decision you can make is that you did it

yesterday I looked up the rue Frémicourt on a map
and was happy to find it like a bird
flying over Paris et ses environs
which unfortunately did not include Seine-et-Oise which I don't know
as well as a number of other things
and Allen is back talking about god a lot
and Peter is back not talking very much
and Joe has a cold and is not coming to Kenneth's
although he is coming to lunch with Norman
I suspect he is making a distinction
well, who isn't

I wish I were reeling around Paris
instead of reeling around New York
I wish I weren't reeling at all
it is Spring the ice has melted the Ricard is being poured
we are all happy and young and toothless
it is the same as old age
the only thing to do is simply continue
is that simple
yes, it is simple because it is the only thing to do
can you do it
yes, you can because it is the only thing to do
blue light over the Bois de Boulogne it continues

the Seine continues
the Louvre stays open it continues it hardly closes at all
the Bar Américain continues to be French
de Gaulle continues to be Algerian as does Camus
Shirley Goldfarb continues to be Shirley Goldfarb
and Jane Hazan continues to be Jane Freilicher (I think!)
and Irving Sandler continues to be the balayeur des artistes
and so do I (sometimes I think I'm "in love" with painting)
and surely the Piscine Deligny continues to have water in it
and the Flore continues to have tables and newspapers and people under them
and surely we shall not continue to be unhappy
we shall be happy
but we shall continue to be ourselves everything continues to be possible
René Char, Pierre Reverdy, Samuel Beckett it is possible isn't it
I love Reverdy for saying yes, though I don't believe it

1959

JOE'S JACKET

Entraining to Southampton in the parlor car with Jap and Vincent, I
see life as a penetrable landscape lit from above
like it was in my Barbizonian kiddy days when automobiles
were owned by the same people for years and the Alfa Romeo was
only a rumor under the leaves beside the viaduct and I
pretending to be adult felt the blue within me and the light up there
no central figure me, I was some sort of cloud or a gust of wind
at the station a crowd of drunken fishermen on a picnic Kenneth
is hard to find but we find, through all the singing, Kenneth smiling
it is off to Janice's bluefish and the incessant talk of affection
expressed as excitability and spleen to be recent and strong
and not unbearably right in attitude, full of confidences
now I will say it, thank god, I knew you would

an enormous party mesmerizing corners in the disgathering light
and dancing miniature-endless, like a pivot
I drink to smother my sensitivity for a while so I won't stare away
I drink to kill the fear of boredom, the mounting panic of it
I drink to reduce my seriousness so a certain spurious charm
can appear and win its flickering little victory over noise
I drink to die a little and increase the contrast of this questionable moment
and then I am going home, purged of everything except anxiety and self-distrust
now I will say it, thank god, I knew you would
and the rain has commenced its delicate lament over the orchards

an enormous window morning and the wind, the beautiful desperation of a tree
fighting off strangulation, and my bed has an ugly calm
I reach to the D. H. Lawrence on the floor and read "The Ship of Death"
I lie back again and begin slowly to drift and then to sink
a somnolent envy of inertia makes me rise naked and go to the window
where the car horn mysteriously starts to honk, no one is there
and Kenneth comes out and stops it in the soft green lightless stare
and we are soon in the Paris of Kenneth's libretto, I did not drift
away I did not die I am there with Haussmann and the rue de Rivoli
and the spirits of beauty, art and progress, pertinent and mobile
in their worldly way, and musical and strange the sun comes out

returning by car the forceful histories of myself and Vincent loom
like the city hour after hour closer and closer to the future I am here
and the night is heavy though not warm, Joe is still up and we talk
only of the immediate present and its indiscriminately hitched-to past
the feeling of life and incident pouring over the sleeping city
which seems to be bathed in an unobtrusive light which lends things
coherence and an absolute, for just that time as four o'clock goes by

and soon I am rising for the less than average day, I have coffee
I prepare calmly to face almost everything that will come up I am calm
but not as my bed was calm as it softly declined to become a ship
I borrow Joe's seersucker jacket though he is still asleep I start out
when I last borrowed it I was leaving there it was on my Spanish plaza back
and hid my shoulders from San Marco's pigeons was jostled on the Kurfürstendamm
and sat opposite Ashes in an enormous leather chair in the Continental
it is all enormity and life it has protected me and kept me here on
many occasions as a symbol does when the heart is full and risks no speech
a precaution I loathe as the pheasant loathes the season and is preserved
it will not be need, it will be just what it is and just what happens

1959

YOU ARE GORGEOUS AND I'M COMING

Vaguely I hear the purple roar of the torn-down Third Avenue El
it sways slightly but firmly like a hand or a golden-downed thigh
normally I don't think of sounds as colored unless I'm feeling corrupt
concrete Rimbaud obscurity of emotion which is simple and very definite
even lasting, yes it may be that dark and purifying wave, the death of boredom
nearing the heights themselves may destroy you in the pure air
to be further complicated, confused, empty but refilling, exposed to light

With the past falling away as an acceleration of nerves thundering and shaking
aims its aggregating force like the Métro towards a realm of encircling travel
rending the sound of adventure and becoming ultimately local and intimate
repeating the phrases of an old romance which is constantly renewed by the
endless originality of human loss the air the stumbling quiet of breathing
newly the heavens' stars all out we are all for the captured time of our being

1959

POEM

The fluorescent tubing burns like a bobby-soxer's ankles
the white paint the green leaves in an old champagne bottle
and the formica shelves going up in the office
and the formica desk-tops over the white floor
what kind of an office is this anyway
I am so nervous about my life the little of it I can get ahold of
so I call up Kenneth in Southampton and presto
he is leaning on the shelf in the kitchen three hours away
while Janice is drying her hair which has prevented her from hearing
my voice through the telephone company ear-blacker
why black a clean ear
Kenneth you are really the backbone of a tremendous poetry nervous system
which keeps sending messages along the wireless luxuriance
of distraught experiences and hysterical desires so to keep things humming
and have nothing go off the trackless tracks
and once more you have balanced me precariously
on the wilderness wish
of wanting to be everything to everybody everywhere
as the vigor of Africa through the corridor
the sands of Sahara still tickle in my jockey shorts
the air-conditioner grunts like that Eskimo dad
and the phone clicks as your glasses bump the receiver
to say we are in America and it is all right not to be elsewhere

1959

"L'AMOUR AVAIT PASSÉ PAR LÀ"

Yes
like the still center of a book on Joan Miró
blue red green and white
a slightly over-gold edition of Hart Crane
and the huge mirror behind me blinking, paint-flecked
they have painted the ceiling of my heart
and put in a new light fixture
and Arte Contemporáneo by Juan Eduardo Cirlot
and the Petit Guide to the Musée National Russe
it is all blankly defending its privacy
from the sighing wind in the ceiling
of the old Theatre Guild building
on West 53rd Street
near the broken promises of casualness
to get to the Cedar to meet Grace
I must tighten my moccasins
and forget the minute bibliographies of disappointment
anguish and power
for unrelaxed honesty
this laissez-passer for chance and misery, but taut
a candle held to the window has two flames
and perhaps a horde of followers in the rain of youth
as under the arch you find a heart of lipstick or a condom
left by the parade
of a generalized intuition
it is the great period of Italian art when everyone imitates Picasso
afraid to mean anything
as the second flame in its happy reflecting ignores the candle and the wind

1959

POEM

Hate is only one of·many responses
true, hurt and hate go hand in hand
but why be afraid of hate, it is only there

think of filth, is it really awesome
neither is hate
don't be shy of unkindness, either
it's cleansing and allows you to be direct
like an arrow that feels something

out and out meanness, too, lets love breathe
you don't have to fight off getting in too deep
you can always get out if you're not too scared

an ounce of prevention's
enough to poison the heart
don't think of others
until you have thought of yourself, are true

all of these things, if you feel them
will be graced by a certain reluctance
and turn into gold

if felt by me, will be smilingly deflected
by your mysterious concern

1959

POEM

I don't know as I get what D. H. Lawrence is driving at
when he writes of lust springing from the bowels
or do I
it could be the bowels of the earth
to lie flat on the earth in spring, summer or winter is sexy
you feel it stirring deep down slowly up to you
and sometimes it gives you a little nudge in the crotch
that's very sexy
and when someone looks sort of raggedy and dirty like Paulette Goddard
in *Modern Times* it's exciting, it isn't usual or attractive
perhaps D.H.L. is thinking of the darkness
certainly the crotch is light
and I suppose
any part of us that can only be seen by others
is a dark part
I feel that about the small of my back, too and the nape of my neck
they are dark
they are erotic zones as in the tropics
whereas Paris is straightforward and bright about it all
a coal miner has kind of a sexy occupation
though I'm sure it's painful down there
but so is lust
of light we can never have enough
but how would we find it
unless the darkness urged us on and into it
and I am dark
except when now and then it all comes clear
and I can see myself
as others luckily sometimes see me
in a good light

1959

PERSONAL POEM

Now when I walk around at lunchtime
I have only two charms in my pocket
an old Roman coin Mike Kanemitsu gave me
and a bolt-head that broke off a packing case
when I was in Madrid the others never
brought me too much luck though they did
help keep me in New York against coercion
but now I'm happy for a time and interested

I walk through the luminous humidity
passing the House of Seagram with its wet
and its loungers and the construction to
the left that closed the sidewalk if
I ever get to be a construction worker
I'd like to have a silver hat please
and get to Moriarty's where I wait for
LeRoi and hear who wants to be a mover and
shaker the last five years my batting average
is .016 that's that, and LeRoi comes in
and tells me Miles Davis was clubbed 12
times last night outside BIRDLAND by a cop
a lady asks us for a nickel for a terrible
disease but we don't give her one we
don't like terrible diseases, then
we go eat some fish and some ale it's
cool but crowded we don't like Lionel Trilling
we decide, we like Don Allen we don't like
Henry James so much we like Herman Melville
we don't want to be in the poets' walk in
San Francisco even we just want to be rich
and walk on girders in our silver hats

I wonder if one person out of the 8,000,000 is
thinking of me as I shake hands with LeRoi
and buy a strap for my wristwatch and go
back to work happy at the thought possibly so

1959

POST THE LAKE POETS BALLAD

Moving slowly sweating a lot
I am pushed by a gentle breeze
outside the Paradise Bar on
      St. Mark's Place and I breathe

and bourbon with Joe he says
did you see a letter from Larry
in the mailbox what a shame I didn't
      I wonder what it says

and then we eat and go to
The Horse Riders and my bum aches
from the hard seats and boredom
      is hard too we don't go

to the Cedar it's so hot out
and I read the letter which says
in your poems your gorgeous self-pity
      how do you like that

that is odd I think of myself
as a cheerful type who pretends to
be hurt to get a little depth into
      things that interest me

and I've even given that up
lately with the stream of events
going so fast and the movingly
      alternating with the amusingly

the depth all in the ocean
although I'm different in the winter
of course even this is a complaint
      but I'm happy anyhow

no more self-pity than Gertrude
Stein before Lucey Church or Savonarola
in the pulpit Allen Ginsberg at the
        Soviet Exposition am I Joe

                                    1959

NAPHTHA

Ah Jean Dubuffet
when you think of him
doing his military service in the Eiffel Tower
as a meteorologist
in 1922
you know how wonderful the 20th Century
can be
and the gaited Iroquois on the girders
fierce and unflinching-footed
nude as they should be
slightly empty
like a Sonia Delaunay
there is a parable of speed
somewhere behind the Indians' eyes
they invented the century with their horses
and their fragile backs
which are dark

we owe a debt to the Iroquois
and to Duke Ellington
for playing in the buildings when they are built
we don't do much ourselves
but fuck and think
of the haunting Métro
and the one who didn't show up there
while we were waiting to become part of our century
just as you can't make a hat out of steel
and still wear it
who wears hats anyway
it is our tribe's custom
to beguile

how are you feeling in ancient September
I am feeling like a truck on a wet highway
how can you
you were made in the image of god
I was not

I was made in the image of a sissy truck-driver
and Jean Dubuffet painting his cows
"with a likeness burst in the memory"
apart from love (don't say it)
I am ashamed of my century
for being so entertaining
but I have to smile

1959

KEIN TRAUM

Awakening, now, the war has broken out
everything is vicious and cruel
as it really is
we are back in reality
out of cigarettes
dying gorgeously
for an unknown principle
as persons we are abstract
and certain
the smoldering snow is falling
as it did when Liszt died
and the Austro-Hungarian empire
was initiating trouble
a lot of trouble
there was a germ of outrageous desire
it lodged in our hearts
it will never succumb it is within us
it will never die
but we shall die
and awaken from our torment
in a storm of anguish
which is just
octaves of war
pound through my willing brain
and everything is right again
we are deciduous
like a dead tree
across this vile street
an old lady in a wig is plucking her eyebrows
in the window
death

1959

POEM

Khrushchev is coming on the right day!
                                        the cool graced light
is pushed off the enormous glass piers by hard wind
and everything is tossing, hurrying on up
                                        this country
has everything but *politesse,* a Puerto Rican cab driver says
and five different girls I see
                                look like Piedie Gimbel
with her blonde hair tossing too,
                                as she looked when I pushed
her little daughter on the swing on the lawn it was also windy

last night we went to a movie and came out,
                                        Ionesco is greater
than Beckett, Vincent said, that's what I think, blueberry blintzes
and Khrushchev was probably being carped at
                                        in Washington, no *politesse*
Vincent tells me about his mother's trip to Sweden
                                        Hans tells us
about his father's life in Sweden, it sounds like Grace Hartigan's
painting *Sweden*
                so I go home to bed and names drift through my head
Purgatorio Merchado, Gerhard Schwartz and Gaspar Gonzales, all
        unknown figures of the early morning as I go to work

where does the evil of the year go
                                when September takes New York
and turns it into ozone stalagmites
                                deposits of light
                                so I get back up
make coffee, and read François Villon, his life, so dark
    New York seems blinding and my tie is blowing up the street
I wish it would blow off
                        though it is cold and somewhat warms my neck

as the train bears Khrushchev on to Pennsylvania Station
    and the light seems to be eternal
    and joy seems to be inexorable
    I am foolish enough always to find it in wind

1959

GETTING UP AHEAD OF SOMEONE (SUN)

I cough a lot (sinus?) so I
get up and have some tea with cognac
it is dawn
             the light flows evenly along the lawn
in chilly Southampton and I smoke
and hours and hours go by I read
van Vechten's *Spider Boy* then a short
story by Patsy Southgate and a poem
by myself it is cold and I shiver a little
in white shorts the day begun
so oddly not tired not nervous I
am for once truly awake letting it all
start slowly as I watch instead of
grabbing on late as usual
                      where did it go
                      it's not really awake yet
                      I will wait

and the house wakes up and goes
to get the dog in Sag Harbor I make
myself a bourbon and commence
to write one of my "I do this I do that"
poems in a sketch pad
                   it is tomorrow
though only six hours have gone by
each day's light has more significance these days

1956

IN FAVOR OF ONE'S TIME

The spent purpose of a perfectly marvellous
life suddenly glimmers and leaps into flame
it's more difficult than you think to make charcoal
it's also pretty hard to remember life's marvellous
but there it is guttering choking then soaring
in the mirrored room of this consciousness
it's practically a blaze of pure sensibility
and however exaggerated at least something's going on
and the quick oxygen in the air will not go neglected
will not sulk or fall into blackness and peat

an angel flying slowly, curiously singes its wings
and you diminish for a moment out of respect
for beauty then flare up after all that's the angel
that wrestled with Jacob and loves conflict
as an athlete loves the tape, and we're off into
an immortal contest of actuality and pride
which is love assuming the consciousness of itself
as sky over all, medium of finding and founding
not just resemblance but the magnetic otherness
that that that stands erect in the spirit's glare
and waits for the joining of an opposite force's breath

so come the winds into our lives and last
longer than despair's sharp snake, crushed before it conquered
so marvellous is not just a poet's greenish namesake
and we live outside his garden in our tempestuous rights

1959

LES LUTHS

Ah nuts! It's boring reading French newspapers
in New York as if I were a Colonial waiting for my gin
somewhere beyond this roof a jet is making a sketch of the sky
where is Gary Snyder I wonder if he's reading under a dwarf pine
stretched out so his book and his head fit under the lowest branch
while the sun of the Orient rolls calmly not getting through to him
not caring particularly because the light in Japan respects poets

while in Paris Monsieur Martory and his brother Jean the poet
are reading a piece by Matthieu Galey and preparing to send a *pneu*
everybody here is running around after dull pleasantries and
wondering if *The Hotel Wentley Poems* is as great as I say it is
and I am feeling particularly testy at being separated from
the one I love by the most dreary of practical exigencies money
when I want only to lean on my elbow and stare into space feeling
the one warm beautiful thing in the world breathing upon my right rib

what are lutes they make ugly twangs and rest on knees in cafés
I want to hear only your light voice running on about Florida
as we pass the changing traffic light and buy grapes for wherever
we will end up praising the mattressless sleigh-bed and the
Mexican egg and the clock that will not make me know
       how to leave you

1959

POEM

to Donald M. Allen

Now the violets are all gone, the rhinoceroses, the cymbals
a grisly pale has settled over the stockyard where the fur flies
and the sound
                is that of a bulldozer in heat stuck in the mud
where a lilac still scrawnily blooms and cries out "Walt!"
so they repair the street in the middle of the night
and Allen and Peter can once again walk forth to visit friends
in the illuminated moonlight over the mists and the towers
having mistakenly thought that Bebe Daniels was in *I Cover the Waterfront*
instead of Claudette Colbert it has begun to rain softly and I walk
slowly thinking of becoming a stalk of asparagus for Hallowe'en
     which idea Vincent poopoos as not being really 40s
so the weight
              of the rain drifting amiably is like a sentimental breeze
and seems to have been invented by a collapsed Kim Novak balloon

yet Janice is helping Kenneth appeal to The Ford Foundation in
her manner oft described as The Sweet Succinct and Ned is glad
       not to be up too late
                     for the sake of his music and his ear
          where discipline finds itself singing and even screaming away

I shall not dine another night like this with Robin and Don and Joe
as lightly as the day is gone but that was earlier
                        a knock on the door
my heart your heart

        my head and the strange reality of our flesh in the rain
so many parts of a strange existence independent but not searching in the night
                nor in the morning when the rain has stopped

1959

POEM

"À la recherche d' Gertrude Stein"

When I am feeling depressed and anxious sullen
all you have to do is take your clothes off
and all is wiped away revealing life's tenderness
that we are flesh and breathe and are near us
as you are really as you are I become as I
really am alive and knowing vaguely what is
and what is important to me above the intrusions
of incident and accidental relationships
which have nothing to do with my life

when I am in your presence I feel life is strong
and will defeat all its enemies and all of mine
and all of yours and yours in you and mine in me
sick logic and feeble reasoning are cured
by the perfect symmetry of your arms and legs
spread out making an eternal circle together
creating a golden pillar beside the Atlantic
the faint line of hair dividing your torso
gives my mind rest and emotions their release
into the infinite air where since once we are
together we always will be in this life come what may

1959

181

POEM

Light   clarity   avocado salad in the morning
after all the terrible things I do how amazing it is
to find forgiveness and love, not even forgiveness
since what is done is done and forgiveness isn't love
and love is love nothing can ever go wrong
though things can get irritating boring and dispensable
(in the imagination) but not really for love
though a block away you feel distant the mere presence
changes everything like a chemical dropped on a paper
and all thoughts disappear in a strange quiet excitement
I am sure of nothing but this, intensified by breathing

1959

HÔTEL TRANSYLVANIE

Shall we win at love or shall we lose
                                    can it be
that hurting and being hurt is a trick forcing the love
we want to appear, that the hurt is a card
and is it black? is it red? is it a paper, dry of tears
chevalier, change your expression! the wind is sweeping over
the gaming tables ruffling the cards/they are black and red
like a Futurist torture and how do you know it isn't always there
waiting while doubt is the father that has you kidnapped by friends

      yet you will always live in a jealous society of accident
you will never know how beautiful you are or how beautiful
the other is, you will continue to refuse to die for yourself
you will continue to sing on trying to cheer everyone up
and they will know as they listen with excessive pleasure that you're dead
and they will not mind that they have let you entertain
at the expense of the only thing you want in the world/you are amusing
as a game is amusing when someone is forced to lose as in a game I must

         oh *hôtel*, you should be merely a bed
surrounded by walls where two souls meet and do nothing but breathe
breathe in breathe out fuse illuminate confuse *stick* dissemble
but not as cheaters at cards have something to win/you have only to be
as you are being, as you must be, as you always are, as you shall be forever
no matter what fate deals you or the imagination discards like a tyrant
as the drums descend and summon the hatchet over the tinselled realities

you know that I am not here to fool around, that I must win or die
I expect you to do everything because it is of no consequence/no duel
you must rig the deck you must make me win at whatever cost to the reputation
of the establishment/sublime moment of dishonest hope/I must win
for if the floods of tears arrive they will wash it all away
                                and then
you will know what it is to want something, but you may not be allowed
to die as I have died, you may only be allowed to drift downstream
to another body of inimical attractions for which you will substitute/distrust

and I will have had my revenge on the black bitch of my nature which you
love as I have never loved myself

but I hold on/I am lyrical to a fault/I do not despair being too foolish
where will you find me, projective verse, since I will be gone?
for six seconds of your beautiful face I will sell the hotel and commit
an uninteresting suicide in Louisiana where it will take them a long time
to know who I am/why I came there/what and why I am and made to happen

1959

[ON THE VAST HIGHWAY]

On the vast highway
where death streams cheerfully
in the sunlight and the enormous spans
cast their 4 o'clock suspensions
over the harbor I am told
of the infidelities of the Puerto Ricans
and the meanness of the Jews
by an Irish cab driver
it is good that there are so many kinds of us
so death can choose
and even perhaps prefer
he who casts the first shadow of the day
on those who are trying to live till dark

1960

PRESENT

The stranded gulch
                below Grand Central
the gentle purr of cab tires in snow
and hidden stars
                    tears on the windshield
torn inexorably away in whining motion
and the dark thoughts which surround neon

in Union Square I see you for a moment
red green yellow searchlights cutting through
falling flakes, head bent to the wind
wet and frowning, melancholy, trying

I know perfectly well where you walk to
and that we'll meet in even greater darkness
later and will be warm
                        so our cross
of paths will not be just muddy footprints
in the morning
                    not like celestial bodies'
yearly passes, nothing pushes us away
from each other
                        even now I can lean
forward across the square and see
your surprised grey look become greener
as I wipe the city's moisture from
your face
              and you shake the snow
off onto my shoulder, light as a breath
where the quarrels and vices of
estranged companions weighed so bitterly
and accidentally
                        before, I saw you on
the floor of my life walking slowly
that time in summer rain stranger and
nearer
              to become a way of feeling

that is not painful casual or diffuse
and seems to explore some peculiar insight
of the heavens for its favorite bodies
in the mixed-up air

                                        1960

POEM

That's not a cross look it's a sign of life
but I'm glad you care how I look at you
this morning (after I got up) I was thinking
of President Warren G. Harding and Horace S.
Warren, father of the little blonde girl
across the street and another blonde Agnes
Hedlund (this was in the 6th grade!)   what

now the day has begun in a soft grey way
with elephantine traffic trudging along Fifth
and two packages of Camels in my pocket
I can't think of one interesting thing Warren
G. Harding did, I guess I was passing notes
to Sally and Agnes at the time he came up
in our elephantine history course everything

seems slow suddenly and boring except
for my insatiable thinking towards you
as you lie asleep completely plotzed and
gracious as a hillock in the mist from one
small window, sunless and only slightly open
as is your mouth and presently your quiet eyes
your breathing is like that history lesson

1960

AVENUE A

We hardly ever see the moon any more
                              so no wonder
   it's so beautiful when we look up suddenly
and there it is gliding broken-faced over the bridges
brilliantly coursing, soft, and a cool wind fans
        your hair over your forehead and your memories
           of Red Grooms' locomotive landscape
I want some bourbon/you want some oranges/I love the leather
           jacket Norman gave me
                              and the corduroy coat David
     gave you, it is more mysterious than spring, the El Greco
heavens breaking open and then reassembling like lions
                              in a vast tragic veldt
     that is far from our small selves and our temporally united
passions in the cathedral of Januaries

     everything is too comprehensible
these are my delicate and caressing poems
I suppose there will be more of those others to come, as in the past
                              so many!
but for now the moon is revealing itself like a pearl
                         to my equally naked heart

                                        1960

NOW THAT I AM IN MADRID AND CAN THINK

I think of you
and the continents brilliant and arid
and the slender heart you are sharing my share of with the American air
as the lungs I have felt sonorously subside slowly greet each morning
and your brown lashes flutter revealing two perfect dawns colored by New York

see a vast bridge stretching to the humbled outskirts with only you
   standing on the edge of the purple like an only tree

and in Toledo the olive groves' soft blue look at the hills with silver
   like glasses like an old lady's hair
it's well known that God and I don't get along together
it's just a view of the brass works to me, I don't care about the Moors
seen through you the great works of death, you are greater

you are smiling, you are emptying the world so we can be alone

1960

A LITTLE TRAVEL DIARY

Wending our way through the gambas, angulas,
the merluzas that taste like the Sea Post on Sunday
and the great quantities of huevos they take off
Spanish Naval officers' uniforms and put on plates,
and reach the gare de Francia in the gloaming
with my ton of books and John's ton of clothes bought
in a wild fit of enthusiasm in Madrid; all jumbled
together like life is a Jumble Shop

                              of the theatre
in Spain they said nothing for foreigners
and we head in our lovely 1st class coach, shifting
and sagging, towards the northwest, while in other compartments
Dietrich and Erich von Stroheim share a sandwich of chorizos
and a bottle of Vichy Catalan, in the dining car
the travelling gentleman with linear mustache and many
many rings rolls his cigar around and drinks Martini y
ginebra, and Lillian Gish rolls on over the gorges
with a tear in her left front eye, comme Picasso,
through the night through the night, longitudinous
and affected with stars; the riverbeds so far below look
as a pig's tongue on a platter, and storms break over
San Sebastian, 40 foot waves drench us pleasantly and we see
a dead dog bloated as a fraise lolling beside the quai
and slowly pulling out to sea

                              to Irún and Biarritz
we go, sapped of anxiety, and there for the first time
since arriving in Barcelona I can freely shit
and the surf is so high and the sun is so hot
and it was all built yesterday as everything should be
what a splendid country it is

          full of indecision and cognac
and bikinis, sens plastiques (ugh! hooray!); see the back
of the head of Bill Berkson, aux Deux Magots, (awk!) it gleams
like the moon through the smoke of the Renfe as we passed
through the endless tunnels and the silver vistas
of our quest for the rocher de la Vierge and salt spray

                                        1960

BEER FOR BREAKFAST

It's the month of May in my heart as the song
says and everything's perfect: a little too chilly
for April and the chestnut trees are refusing to bloom
as they should refuse if they don't want to, sky
clear and blue with a lot of side-paddle steamers
pushing through to Stockholm where the canals're true-blue

in my spacious quarters on the rue de l'Université
I give a cocktail in the bathroom, everyone gets wet
it's very beachy; and I clear my head staring at the sign
LOI DU 29 JUILLET 1881
                                   so capitalizing on a few memories
from childhood by forgetting them, I'm happy as a finger
of Vermouth being poured over a slice of veal, it's
the new reality in the city of Balzac! praying to be let
into the cinema and become an influence, carried through
streets on the shoulders of Messrs Chabrol and Truffaut
towards Nice
                    or do you think that the Golden Lion
would taste pleasanter (not with vermouth, lion!)?
no, but San Francisco, maybe, and abalone

                                                  there is
nothing in the world I wouldn't do foryouforyou (zip!)
and I go off to meet Mario and Marc at the Flore

                                                            1960

HAVING A COKE WITH YOU

is even more fun than going to San Sebastian, Irún, Hendaye, Biarritz, Bayonne
or being sick to my stomach on the Travesera de Gracia in Barcelona
partly because in your orange shirt you look like a better happier St. Sebastian
partly because of my love for you, partly because of your love for yoghurt
partly because of the fluorescent orange tulips around the birches
partly because of the secrecy our smiles take on before people and statuary
it is hard to believe when I'm with you that there can be anything as still
as solemn as unpleasantly definitive as statuary when right in front of it
in the warm New York 4 o'clock light we are drifting back and forth
between each other like a tree breathing through its spectacles

and the portrait show seems to have no faces in it at all, just paint
you suddenly wonder why in the world anyone ever did them
                                                        I look
at you and I would rather look at you than all the portraits in the world
except possibly for the *Polish Rider* occasionally and anyway it's in the Frick
which thank heavens you haven't gone to yet so we can go together the first time
and the fact that you move so beautifully more or less takes care of Futurism
just as at home I never think of the *Nude Descending a Staircase* or
at a rehearsal a single drawing of Leonardo or Michelangelo that used to wow me
and what good does all the research of the Impressionists do them
when they never got the right person to stand near the tree when the sun sank
or for that matter Marino Marini when he didn't pick the rider as carefully
as the horse
            it seems they were all cheated of some marvellous experience
which is not going to go wasted on me which is why I'm telling you about it

1960

STEPS

How funny you are today New York
like Ginger Rogers in *Swingtime*
and St. Bridget's steeple leaning a little to the left

here I have just jumped out of a bed full of V-days
(I got tired of D-days) and blue you there still
accepts me foolish and free
all I want is a room up there
and you in it
and even the traffic halt so thick is a way
for people to rub up against each other
and when their surgical appliances lock
they stay together
for the rest of the day (what a day)
I go by to check a slide and I say
that painting's not so blue

where's Lana Turner
she's out eating
and Garbo's backstage at the Met
everyone's taking their coat off
so they can show a rib-cage to the rib-watchers
and the park's full of dancers with their tights and shoes
in little bags
who are often mistaken for worker-outers at the West Side Y
why not
the Pittsburgh Pirates shout because they won
and in a sense we're all winning
we're alive

the apartment was vacated by a gay couple
who moved to the country for fun
they moved a day too soon
even the stabbings are helping the population explosion
though in the wrong country
and all those liars have left the U N

the Seagram Building's no longer rivalled in interest
not that we need liquor (we just like it)

and the little box is out on the sidewalk
next to the delicatessen
so the old man can sit on it and drink beer
and get knocked off it by his wife later in the day
while the sun is still shining

oh god it's wonderful
to get out of bed
and drink too much coffee
and smoke too many cigarettes
and love you so much

1960

AVE MARIA

Mothers of America
                    let your kids go to the movies!
get them out of the house so they won't know what you're up to
it's true that fresh air is good for the body
                                but what about the soul
that grows in darkness, embossed by silvery images
and when you grow old as grow old you must
                                they won't hate you
they won't criticize you they won't know
                                they'll be in some glamorous country
they first saw on a Saturday afternoon or playing hookey

they may even be grateful to you
                        for their first sexual experience
which only cost you a quarter
                        and didn't upset the peaceful home
they will know where candy bars come from
                                and gratuitous bags of popcorn
as gratuitous as leaving the movie before it's over
with a pleasant stranger whose apartment is in the Heaven on Earth Bldg
near the Williamsburg Bridge
                        oh mothers you will have made the little tykes
so happy because if nobody does pick them up in the movies
they won't know the difference
                        and if somebody does it'll be sheer gravy
and they'll have been truly entertained either way
instead of hanging around the yard
                        or up in their room
                                hating you
prematurely since you won't have done anything horribly mean yet
except keeping them from the darker joys

                                        it's unforgivable the latter
so don't blame me if you won't take this advice
                                        and the family breaks up
and your children grow old and blind in front of a TV set
                                        seeing
movies you wouldn't let them see when they were young

                                                            1960

FOND SONORE

In placing this particular thought
I am taking up the cudgel against indifference
I wish that I might be different but I am
that I am is all I have so what can I do

as the hero of the hour I might have one strange destiny
but it is all mixed up and I have several
I can't choose between them they are pulling me aloft
which is not to say up like a Baroque ceiling or anything

where is the rain and the lightning to drown or burn us
as there used to be
where are the gods who could abuse and disabuse us often
when am I ever in the country walking along a lane plotting murder

you would think that the best things in life were free
but they're the worst even the air is dirty
and it's this "filth of life" that coats us against pain
so where are we back at the same old stand buying bagels

I think that it would be nice to go away
but that's reserved for TV and who wants to end up in Paradise
it's not our milieu
we would be lost as a fish is lost when it has to swim

and yet and yet
this place is terrible to see and worse to feel
along with the purple you have contracted for an awful virus
and it is Christmas and the children are growing up

1960

[THE FONDEST DREAM OF]

The fondest dream of
every American boy
is to go to work and use
his father's typewriter

you spill ink over
his secretary and follow her
to the fainting room
where she fails to wash it off

1960

CORNKIND

So the rain falls
it drops all over the place
and where it finds a little rock pool
it fills it up with dirt
and the corn grows
a green Bette Davis sits under it
reading a volume of William Morris
oh fertility! beloved of the Western world
you aren't so popular in China
though they fuck too

and do I really want a son
to carry on my idiocy past the Horned Gates
poor kid   a staggering load

yet it can happen casually
and he lifts a little of the load each day
as I become more and more idiotic
and grows to be a strong strong man
and one day carries as I die
my final idiocy and the very gates
into a future of his choice

but what of William Morris
what of you Million Worries
what of Bette Davis in
AN EVENING WITH WILLIAM MORRIS
or THE WORLD OF SAMUEL GREENBERG

what of Hart Crane
what of phonograph records and gin

what of "what of"

you are of me, that's what
and that's the meaning of fertility
hard and moist and moaning

1960

MACARONI

to Patsy Southgate

Voici la clématite around the old door
which I planted, watered, and let die
as I have with so many cats, although *sans une claire-voie*
and it seemed that the whole summer dipped
when it withered, when the leaves did, and the purple
blossoms lingered as if you could smell them eventually

on ne vit pas par l'essence seule, thank you
Patsy, for the dope on *essence de vie* and if I'm not
asleep I'll come tonight to talk about
the old days when my father knocked me into the rose-bed
thereby killing a half dozen of his prized rose plants
yak, yak it's a wonderful life for the plants

when you think of what Shelley did with such a theme
and long afterwards Mallarmé reciting it to himself
far across the channel in all that loneliness and stren'th
you wonder if I shouldn't be back on the phone getting black ear
don't you? well, back to your novel, wench! *assez*

you and Marisol, the Grace Kelly and Maria Callas
of the New York School, I do wish that clematis had growed
I don't know what happened, I guess I just lost interest
which along with the current recession fills me with guilt
and besides I was a kid, as now I can hardly be made responsible
for the money troubles of our nation, almost never
having seen any, but the plant in your life

is the plant that died, *"mourir, c'est ainsi pousser"*

1961

FOR THE CHINESE NEW YEAR & FOR BILL BERKSON

One or another
Is lost, since we fall apart
Endlessly, in one motion depart
From each other.

—D.H. LAWRENCE

Behind New York there's a face
and it's not Sibelius's with a cigar
it was red it was strange and hateful
and then I became a child again
like a nadir or a zenith or a nudnik

what do you think this is my youth
and the aged future that is sweeping me away
carless and gasless under the Sutton
and Beekman Places towards a hellish rage
it is there that face I fear under ramps

it is perhaps the period that ends
the problem as a proposition of days of days
just an attack on the feelings that stay
poised in the hurricane's center that
eye through which only camels can pass

but I do not mean that tenderness doesn't
linger like a Paris afternoon or a wart
something dumb and despicable that I love
because it is silent oh what difference
does it make me into some kind of space statistic

a lot is buried under that smile
a lot of sophistication gone down the drain
to become the mesh of a mythical fish
at which we never stare back never stare back
where there is so much downright forgery

under that I find it restful like a bush
some people are outraged by cleanliness
I hate the lack of smells myself and yet I stay
it is better than being actually present
and the stare can swim away into the past

can adorn it with easy convictions rat
cow tiger rabbit dragon snake horse sheep
monkey rooster dog and pig "Flower Drum Song"
so that nothing is vain not the gelded sand
not the old spangled lotus not my fly

which I have thought about but never really
looked at well that's a certain orderliness
of personality "if you're brought up Protestant
enough a Catholic" oh shit on the beaches so
what if I did look up your trunks and see it

        II
then the parallel becomes an eagle parade
of Busby Berkeleyites marching marching half-toe
I suppose it's the happiest moment in infinity
because we're dissipated and tired and fond no
I don't think psychoanalysis shrinks the spleen

here we are and what the hell are we going to do
with it we are going to blow it up like daddy did
only us I really think we should go up for a change
I'm tired of always going down what price glory
it's one of those timeless priceless words like come

well now how does your conscience feel about that
would you rather explore tomorrow with a sponge
there's no need to look for a target you're it
like in childhood when the going was aimed at a
sandwich it all depends on which three of us are there

but here come the prophets with their loosening nails
it is only as blue as the lighting under the piles
I have something portentous to say to you but which
of the papier-mâché languages do you understand you
don't dare to take it off paper much less put it on

yes it is strange that everyone fucks and every
one mentions it and it's boring too that faded floor
how many teeth have chewed a little piece of the lover's
flesh how many teeth are there in the world it's like
Harpo Marx smiling at a million pianos call that Africa

call it New Guinea call it Poughkeepsie I guess
it's love I guess the season of renunciation is at "hand"
the final fatal hour of turpitude and logic demise
is when you miss getting rid of something delouse
is when you don't louse something up which way is the inn

III
I'm looking for a million-dollar heart in a carton
of frozen strawberries like the Swedes where is sunny England
and those fields where they stillbirth the wars why
did they suddenly stop playing why is Venice a Summer
Festival and not New York were you born in America

the inscrutable passage of a lawn mower punctuates
the newly installed Muzak in the Shubert Theatre am I nuts
or is this the happiest moment of my life who's arguing it's
I mean 'tis lawd sakes it took daddy a long time to have
that accident so Ant Grace could get completely into black

didn't you know we was all going to be Zen Buddhists after
what we did you sure don't know much about war-guilt
or nothin and the peach trees continued to rejoice around
the prick which was for once authorized by our Congress
though inactive what if it had turned out to be a volcano

that's a mulatto of another nationality of marble
it's time for dessert I don't care what street this is
you're not telling me to take a tour are you
I don't want to look at any fingernails or any toes
I just want to go on being subtle and dead like life

I'm not naturally so detached but I think
they might send me up any minute so I try to be free
you know we've all sinned a lot against science
so we really ought to be available as an apple on a bough
pleasant thought fresh air free love cross-pollenization

oh oh god how I'd love to dream let alone sleep it's night
the soft air wraps me like a swarm it's raining and I have
a cold I am a real human being with real ascendancies
and a certain amount of rapture what do you do with a kid
like me if you don't eat me I'll have to eat myself

it's a strange curse my "generation" has we're all
like the flowers in the Agassiz Museum perpetually ardent
don't touch me because when I tremble it makes a noise
like a Chinese wind-bell it's that I'm seismographic is all
and when a Jesuit has stared you down for ever after you clink

I wonder if I've really scrutinized this experience like
you're supposed to have if you can type there's not much
soup left on my sleeve energy creativity guts ponderableness
lent is coming in imponderableness "I'd like to die smiling" ugh
and a very small tiptoe is crossing the threshold away

whither Lumumba whither oh whither Gauguin
I have often tried to say goodbye to strange fantoms I
read about in the newspapers and have always succeeded
though the ones at "home" are dependent on Dependable
Laboratory and Sales Company on Pulaski Street strange

I think it's goodbye to a lot of things like Christmas
and the Mediterranean and halos and meteorites and villages
full of damned children well it's goodbye then as in Strauss
or some other desperately theatrical venture it's goodbye
to lunch to love to evil things and to the ultimate good as "well"

the strange career of a personality begins at five and ends
forty minutes later in a fog the rest is just a lot of stranded
ships honking their horns full of joy-seeking cadets in bloomers
and beards it's okay with me but must they cheer while they honk
it seems that breath could easily fill a balloon and drift away

scaring the locusts in the straggling grey of living dumb
exertions then the useful noise would come of doom of data
turned to elegant decoration like a strangling prince once ordered
no there is no precedent of history no history nobody came before
nobody will ever come before and nobody ever was that man

you will not die not knowing this is true this year

1961

ESSAY ON STYLE

Someone else's Leica sitting on the table
the black kitchen table I am painting
the floor yellow, Bill is painting it
wouldn't you know my mother would call
up
      and complain?
                    my sister's pregnant and
went to the country for the weekend without
telling her
             in point of fact why don't I
go out to have dinner with her or "let her"
come in? well if Mayor Wagner won't allow private
cars on Manhattan because of the snow, I
will probably never see her again
                        considering
my growingly more perpetual state and how
can one say that angel in the Frick's wings
are "attached" if it's a real angel? now

I was reflecting the other night meaning
I was being reflected upon that Sheridan Square
is remarkably beautiful, sitting in JACK
DELANEY's looking out the big race-track window
on the wet
            drinking a cognac while Edwin
read my new poem it occurred to me how impossible
it is to fool Edwin not that I don't know as
much as the next about obscurity in modern verse
but he
          always knows what it's about as well
as what it is do you think we can ever
strike *as* and *but,* too, out of the language
then we can attack *well* since it has no
application whatsoever neither as a state
of being or a rest for the mind no such
things available
             where do you think I've

got to? the spectacle of a grown man
decorating
        a Christmas tree disgusts me that's
where
      that's one of the places yetbutaswell
I'm glad I went to that party for Ed Dorn
last night though he didn't show up do you think
,Bill, we can get rid of *though* also, and *also*?
maybe your
         lettrism is the only answer treating
the typewriter as an intimate organ why not?
nothing else is (intimate)
          no I am not going
to have you "in" for dinner nor am I going "out"
I am going to eat alone for the rest of my life

1961

VINCENT AND I INAUGURATE A MOVIE THEATRE

Now that the Charles Theatre has opened
it looks like we're going to have some wonderful times
Allen and Peter, why are you going away
our country's black and white past spread out
before us is no time to spread over India
like last night in the busy balcony I see
your smoky images before the smoky screen
everyone smoking, Bogart, Bacall and her advanced sister
and Hepburn too tense to smoke but MacMurray rich enough
relaxed and ugly, poor Alice Adams so in-pushed and out
in the clear exposition of AP American or Associated
Paranoia and Allen and I getting depressed and angry
becoming again the male version of wallflower or wallpaper
or something while Vincent points out that when anything
good happens the movie has just flicked over to fantasy
only fantasy in all America can be good
because all Alice Adams wanted was a nose
just as long as any other girl's and a dress
just as rustly and a mind just as empty so America
could fill it with checks and flags and invitations
and the old black cooks falling down the cellar stairs
for generations to show how phony it all is
but the whites didn't pay attention that's slaving away
at something, maybe the dance would have been fun
if anyone'd given one but it would have been over
before Alice enjoyed it and what's the difference
no wonder you want to find out about India take
a print of *Alice Adams* with you it will cheer them up

1961

EARLY ON SUNDAY

It's eight in the morning
everyone has left
the *New York Times* had put itself to bed on Wednesday
or Thursday and arrived
this morning I feel pale
and read the difference between the Masai and the Kikuyu
one keeps and identifies
the other keeps and learns
"newfangledness" in Wyatt's time was not a virtue was it
or should I get up
go out into the Polish sunlight
and riot in Washington Square with Joan with the "folk"
if you like singing
what happened to the clavichord

with hot dogs peanuts and pigeons where's the clavichord
though it's raining
I'm not afraid for the string
they have their hats on across the street in the dirty window
leaning on elbows
without any pillows
how sad the lower East side is on Sunday morning in May
eating yellow eggs
eating St. Bridget's benediction
washing the world down with rye and Coca-Cola and the news
Joe stumbles home
pots and pans crash to the floor
everyone's happy again

1961

ST. PAUL AND ALL THAT

Totally abashed and smiling

> I walk in
> sit down and
> face the frigidaire

> it's April
> no May
> it's May

such little things have to be established in morning
after the big things of night

> do you want me to come? when

I think of all the things I've been thinking of I feel insane
simply "life in Birmingham is hell"

> simply "you will miss me
> but that's good"

when the tears of a whole generation are assembled
they will only fill a coffee cup

> just because they evaporate

doesn't mean life has heat

> "this various dream of living"

I am alive with you

> full of anxious pleasures and pleasurable anxiety

hardness and softness

> listening while you talk and talking while you read

I read what you read

> you do not read what I read

which is right, I am the one with the curiosity
you read for some mysterious reason

> I read simply because I am a writer

the sun doesn't necessarily set, sometimes it just disappears
when you're not here someone walks in and says

> "hey,

there's no dancer in that bed"
                              O the Polish summers! those drafts!
                              those black and white teeth!
you never come when you say you'll come but on the other hand you do come

                                                    1961

I'm getting tired of not wearing underwear
and then again I like it
                        strolling along
feeling the wind blow softly on my genitals
though I also like them encased in something
firm, almost tight, like a projectile
                                at
a streetcorner I stop and a lamppost is
bending over the traffic pensively like a
praying mantis, not lighting anything,
just looking
                  who dropped that empty carton
of cracker jacks I wonder I find the favor
that's a good sign
                it's the blue everyone
is talking about an enormous cloud which hides
the observatory blimp   when you
ride on a 5th Avenue bus you hide on a 5th
Avenue bus I mean compared to you walking
don't hide   there you are trying
to hide behind a fire hydrant   I'm
not going to the Colisseum I'm going to
the Russian Tea Room fooled you didn't I
well   it is nicer in the Park
with the pond and all that   okay
lake   and bicyclists give you
a feeling of being at leisure in the open
air lazy and good-tempered   which is
fairly unusual these days   I liked
for instance   carrying my old Gautier book
and *L'Ombra* over to LeRoi's the other
pale afternoon through the crowds of 3rd
Avenue and the ambulance and the drunk

1961

POEM EN FORME DE SAW

I ducked out of sight behind the sawmill
nobody saw me because of the falls the gates the sluice the tourist boats
the children were trailing their fingers in the water
and the swans, regal and smarty, were nipping their "little" fingers
I heard one swan remark "That was a good nip
though they are not as interesting as sausages" and another
reply "Nor as tasty as those peasants we got away from the elephant that time"
but I didn't really care for conversation that day
I wanted to be alone
which is why I went to the mill in the first place
now I am alone and hate it
I don't want to just make boards for the rest of my life
I'm distressed
the water is very beautiful but you can't go into it
because of the gunk
and the dog is always rolling over, I like dogs on their "little" feet
I think I may scamper off to Winnipeg to see Raymond
but what'll happen to the mill
I see the cobwebs collecting already
and later those other webs, those awful predatory webs
if I stay right here I will eventually get into the newspapers
like Robert Frost
willow trees, willow trees they remind me of Desdemona
I'm so damned literary
and at the same time the waters rushing past remind me of nothing
I'm so damned empty
what is all this vessel shit anyway
we are all rushing down the River Happy Times
ducking poling bumping sinking and swimming
and we arrive at the beach
the chaff is sand
alone as a tree bumping another tree in a storm
that's not really being alone, is it, signed The Saw

1961

METAPHYSICAL POEM

When do you want to go
I'm not sure I want to go there
where do you want to go
any place
I think I'd fall apart any place else
well I'll go if you really want to
I don't particularly care
but you'll fall apart any place else
I can just go home
I don't really mind going there
but I don't want to force you to go there
you won't be forcing me I'd just as soon
I wouldn't be able to stay long anyway
maybe we could go somewhere nearer
I'm not wearing a jacket
just like you weren't wearing a tie
well I didn't say we had to go
I don't care whether you're wearing one
we don't really have to do anything
well all right let's not
okay I'll call you
yes call me

1962

BIOTHERM (FOR BILL BERKSON)

The best thing in the world   but I better be quick about it
better be gone tomorrow

                  better be gone last night and
        next Thursday better be gone
better be

          always   or what's the use the sky
     the endless clouds trailing we leading them by the bandanna, red

you meet the Ambassador   "a year and a half of trying to make him"
     he is dressed in red, he has a red ribbon down his chest he
        has 7   gold decorations pinned to his gash
he sleeps a lot, thinks a lot, fucks a lot, impenetrable and Jude-ish
     I love him, you would love him too   if you could see outside

              whoops-musicale (sei tu m'ami) ahhahahahaha
              loppy di looploop   which is why   I suppose
   Leontyne Price asked Secretary Goldberg to intervene with Metropera
it's not as dangerous as you think
                  NEVERTHELESS (thank you, Aristotle)

    I know you are interested in the incongruities of my behavior, John
just as Bill you are interested in the blue paint JA Oscar Maxine Khnute
perhaps you'd better be particularly interested   POOF

                         extended vibrations
ziggurats ZIG I to IV   stars of the Tigris-Euphrates basin
   leading ultimates such as kickapoo joyjuice halvah Canton cheese
in thimbles
            paraded for gain, but yet a parade kiss me,
                   Busby Berkeley, kiss me
you have ended the war by simply singing in your Irene Dunne foreskin
"Practically Yours"
         with June Vincent, Lionello Venturi and Casper Citron

a Universal-International release produced by G. Mennen Williams
directed by Florine Stettheimer
continuity by the Third Reich
after "hitting" the beach at Endzoay we drank up the liebfraumilch
and pushed on up the Plata to the pampas
you didn't pick up the emeralds you god-damned fool you got
no collarbone you got no dish no ears
Maurice Prendergast
Tilly Losch
"when the seizure tuck 'im 'e went"—Colette
besides, the snow was snowing, our fault for calling the ticket
perhaps at the end of a very strange game
you won   ? (?) ! (?)
and that is important (yeah) to win (yeah)

bent on his knees the Old Mariner said where the fuck
is that motel you told me about mister I aint come here for no clams
I want swimmingpool mudpacks the works carbonateddrugstorewater hiccups
fun a nice sissy under me clean and whistling a donkey to ride rocks
"OKAY (smile) COMING UP"
"This is, after all," said Margaret Dumont, "the *original* MAIN CHANCE"

(fart) "Suck this," said the Old M, spitting on his high heels
which he had just put on to get his navel up to her knee

but even that extended a little further,
out into the desert, where
no flash tested, no flashed!
oops! and no nail polish, yak
yak, yak, Lieut.
no flesh to taste no flash to tusk
no flood to flee no fleed to dlown from the iceth loot
"par exemple!"

out of the dark a monster appears full of grizzly odors which exhale through
him like a samovar belches out the news of the Comintern in a novel by
Howard Fast
        BUT

                  the cuckoo keeps falling off the branch so everything's okay
nobody worries about mistakes disasters calamities so long as they're "natural"
sun sun bene bene bullshit   it's important to be sensitive in business and
insensitive in love because what have you if you have no "balls" what made
the French important after all if not: jeu de balles, pas de balles and,
for murderers of Algerians, règle de balles   may I ask
                  "do you love it?"

   I don't think I want to win anything I think I want to die unadorned

              the dulcet waves are
              sweeping along in their purplish
              way and a little girl is
              beginning to cry and I know
              her but I can't help because
              she has just found her first brick
              what can you do what

does that seem a little too Garboesque? now Garbo, a strange case. oh god

keeping them alive
              there are more waves with bricks in them than there are
                      well-advertised mansions in the famous House
but we will begin again, won't we
                      well I will anyway or as 12,
    "continuez, même stupide garçon"

        "This dedelie stroke, wherebye shall seace
         The harborid sighis within my herte"

and at the doorway there is no

                              acceptable bong except stick mush
room for paranoia comme à l'heure de midi moins quatre
                                                    et pour
JOUR DE FÊTE j'ai composé mon "Glorification" hommage au poète américain
                        lyrique et profond, Wallace Stevens
                                                    but one
                of your American tourists told me he was a banker
                                        quels délices
                I would like to tell you what I think about bankers but . . .
                        except W. C. Fields
what do you want from a bank but love   ouch
                but I don't get any love from Wallace Stevens no I don't
I think délices is a lot of horseshit and that comes from one who infinitely
                                                prefers bullshit
                                        and the bank rolled on
                                        and Stevens strolled on
                                        an ordinary evening alone
                                        with a lot of people

                        "the flow'r you once threw at me
                        socked me with hit me over the head avec
                        has been a real blessing let me think
                        while lying here with the lice
                                            you're a dream"

AND

                        "measure shmeasure know shknew
                        unless the material rattle us around
                        pretty rose preserved in biotherm
                        and yet the y bothers us when we dance
                                            the pussy pout"
                                    never liked to sing much but that's what being
                                        a child means   BONG

le bateleur! how wonderful
I'm so so so so so so so so so so happy

                                                                            221

so happy I make you happy
like in the s- s- s- s- soap opera wow
      what else I mean what else do you need (I)
                                        then you
                 were making me happy otherwise I
                 was staring into *Saturday Night* and flag
                 pink shirt with holes cinzano-soda-grin
                 unh. it is just too pleasant to b.w.y.

hey! help! come back! you spilled your omelette all over your pants!
oh damn it, I guess that's the end of one of our meetings

"vass hass der mensch geplooped
that there is sunk in the battlefield a stately grunt
and the idle fluice still playing on the hill
because of this this this this slunt"
                            it's a secret told by
                            a madman in a parlor car
                            signifying chuckles
                                * Richard Widmark *
                                * Gene Tierney *
                                * Googie Withers *

      I hate the hat you are not wearing, I love to see your narrow head

there in the dark London streets
                         there were all sorts of murderers
                 gamblers and Greek wrestlers
              "I could have had all of wrestling in London in my hand"
                    BANG
                          down by the greasy Thames shack
                          stumbling up and over

      (PROKOFIEVIANA)

One day   you are posing in your checkerboard bathing trunks
      the bear eats only honey   what a strange life

is the best of mine impossible   what does it mean

            that equally strange smile it's like seeing the moon rise
                "keep believing it"
       you will not want, from me

   where you were no longer exists
   which is why we will go see it to be close to you how could it leave
I would never leave you
if I didn't have to
            you will have to too
            Soviet society taught us that
            is the necessity to be "realistic" love is a football
                   I only hear the pianos
       when possession turns into frustration
       the North Star goes out will it
       is there anyone there
the seismograph at Fordham University says it will
                   so it will not

           we are alone no one is talking it feels good
      we have our usual contest about claustrophobia
      it doesn't matter much
      doing without each other is much more insane

           okay, it's not the sun setting it's the moon rising
           I see it that way too

      (BACK TO SATIE)

when the *Vitalità nell' arte* catalog came in the mail I laughed
      thinking it was *Perspectives USA* but it wasn't it
      was vitality nellie arty ho ho that's a joke pop

"I never had to see I just kept looking at the pictures"
damn good show!
don't I know it?
take off your glasses
you're breaking my frame
sculptresses wear dresses

Lo! the Caracas transport lunch with George Al Leslie 5:30 I'll
be over at 5
I hope you will I'm dying of loneliness
here with my red blue green and natch pencils and the erasers
with the mirror behind me and the desk in front of me
like an anti-Cocteau movement
"who did you have lunch with?" "you" "oops!" how ARE you

then too, the other day I was walking through a train
with my suitcase and I overheard someone say "speaking of faggots"
now isn't life difficult enough without that
and why am I always carrying something
well it was a shitty looking person anyway
better a faggot than a farthead
or as fathers have often said to friends of mine
"better dead than a dope" "if I thought you were queer I'd kill you"
you'd be right to, DAD, daddio, addled annie pad-lark (Brit. 19 c.)

well everything can't be perfect
you said it

I definitely do not think that Lobelia would be a suitable name
for Carey and Norman's daughter if they have a daughter
and if they have a son Silverrod is insupportable by most
put that back in your pipe Patsy and make pot out of it honey

you were there I was here you were here I was there where are you I miss you
(that was an example of the "sonnet" "form") (this is another)
when you went I stayed and then I went and we were both lost and then I died

oh god what joy
you're here
sob and at the
most recent summit
conference they
are eating string
beans butter
smootch slurp
pass me the filth
and a coke pal
oh thank you

down at the box-office of Town Hall I was thinking of you in your no hat
    music often reminds me of nothing, that way, like reforming

September 15 (supine, unshaven, hungover, passive, softspoken) I was
very happy
                on Altair 4, I love you that way, it was on Altair 4 "a happy day"
                I knew it would be
                yes to everything
                                I think you will find the pot in the corner
                where the Krells left it
                                        rub it a little and music comes out
                the music of the fears
                                        I reformed we reformed each other
                being available
                                it is something our friends don't understand
                if you loosen your tie
                                        my heart will leap out
                like a Tanagra sculpture
                                        from the crater of the Corsican "lip"
                and flying through the heavens
                                        I am reminded of Kit Carson
                and all those smiles which were exactly like yours
                but we hadn't met yet
                                        when are you going away on "our" trip

why are you melancholy

                        if I make you angry you are no longer doubtful

      if I make you happy you are no longer doubtful

                            what's wrong with doubt

it is mostly that your face
is like the sky behind the Sherry Netherland
blue instead of air, touching instead of remote, warm instead of racing
you are as intimate as a "cup" of vodka

             and when yesterday arrives and troubles us you always say NO
             I don't believe you at first but you say no no no no
             and pretty soon I am smiling and doing just what I want
             again

                 that's very important
                 you put the shit back in the drain
                 and then you actually find the stopper

take back September 15 to Aug something
I think you are wonderful on your birthday

                      I think you are wonderful

      on all your substitute birthdays

                I am rather irritated at your being born
                   at all
               where did you put that stopper
           you are the biggest fool I ever laid eyes on
            that's what they thought about the Magi, I believe

first you peel the potatoes
then you marinate the peelies
in campari all the while playing
the Mephisto Waltz on your gram
and wrap them in grape leaves
and bake them in mush ouch
that god damn oven delicacies
the ditch is full of after dinner

what sky
out there in between the ailanthuses
a 17th Century prison an aardvark
a photograph of Mussolini and
a personal letter from Isak Dinesen
written after eating

the world of thrills! 7 Lively Arts! Week-in-Review! whew!
if you lie there asleep on the floor after lunch
what else is there for me to do but adore you
I am sitting on top of Mauna Loa seeing thinking feeling
the breeze rustles through the mountain gently trusts me
I am guarding it from mess and measure

it is cool
I am high
and happy
as it turns
on the earth
tangles me
in the air

the celestial drapery salutes an ordinary occurrence
the moon is rising I am always thinking of the moon rising

I am always thinking of you
your morality your carved lips
on the beach we stood on our heads
I held your legs it was summer and hot
the Bloody Marys were spilling on our trunks
but the crocodiles didn't pull them
it was a charmed life full of
innuendos and desirable hostilities
I wish we were back there among the
irritating grasses and the helmet crabs
the spindrift gawk towards Swan Lake Allegra Kent
those Ten Steps of Patricia Wilde
unison matches anxious putty Alhambra
bus-loads of Russians' dignity desire

when we meet we smile in another language

you don't know the half of it
I never said I did
your mortality
I am very serious

ENDGAME WAITING FOR GODOT WATT HAPPY DAYS which means I love you
what is that hat doing on that table in my room where I am asleep
"thank you for the dark and the shoulders"
"oh   thank you"

okay I'll meet you at the weather station at 5
we'll take a helicopter into the "eye" of the storm
we'll be so happy in the center of things at last
now the wind rushes up nothing happens and departs
L'EUROPA LETTERATURA CINEMATOGRAFICA ARTISTICA 9-10

your back the street   solidity   fragility erosion
why did this Jewish hurricane have to come
and ruin our Yom Kippur

favorites: vichyssoise, capers, bandannas, fudge-nut-ice, collapsibility,
the bar of the Winslow, 5:30 and 12:30, leather sweaters, tunafish,
cinzano and soda, Marjorie Rambeau in Inspiration
                              whatdoyoumeanandhowdoyoumeanit

(MENU)
Déjeuner Bill Berkson
30 August 1961

Hors-d'oeuvre abstrait-expressionistes, américain-styles, bord-durs, etc.
Soupe Samedi Soir à la Strawberry-Blonde
Poisson Pas de Dix au style Patricia
Histoire de contrefilet, sauce Angelicus Fobb
La réunion des fins de thon à la boue

Chapon ouvert brûlé à l'Hoban, sauce Fidelio Fobb
Poèmes 1960–61 en salade

        Fromage de la Tour Dimanche 17 septembre
        Fruits des Jardins shakspériens
        Biscuits de *l'Inspiration* de Clarence Brown

Vin blanc supérieur de Bunkie Hearst
Vin rouge mélancholique de Boule de neige
Champagne d'*Art News* éditeur diapré
Café ivesianien "Plongez au fond du lac glacé"
                  Vodka-campari et TV

as the clouds parted the New York City Ballet opened Casey Stengel was there
with Blanche Yurka, "Bones" Mifflin, Vera-Ellen and Alice Pearce, Stuts
"Bearcat" Lonklin and Louella "Prudential" Parsons in another "box," Elsa
"I-Don't-Believe-You're-a-Rothschild" Maxwell wouldn't speak to them
because she wasn't "in" the party and despite the general vulgarity Diana
Adams again looked exactly like the moon as she appears in the works of
Alfred de Musset and me
               who am I? I am the floorboards of that zonked palace

after the repast the reap (hic) the future is always fustian (ugh)
    nobody is Anglican everybody is anguished

"now the past is something else the past is like a future that came through
you can remember everything accurately and be proud of your honesty you can
lie about everything that happened and be happily reminiscent you can alter
here and there for increased values you can truly misremember and have it
both ways or you can forget everything completely the past is really something"

        but the future always falls through!
        for instance will I ever really go live
        in Providence Rhode Island or Paestum Lucania
        I doubt it   "you are a rose, though?" (?)

a long history of populations, though
the phrase beginning with "Palms!" and quickly forgotten
in the pit under the dark there were books
being written about strange rites of the time
the time was called The Past and the books were in German
which scholars took to be Sanskrit or Urdu
(much laughter) which later turned out to be indeed
Sanskrit or Urdu (end of laughter, start of fight)
and at the same time the dark was going on and on
never getting bluer or greener or purpler just
going on and that was civilization and still is
nobody could see the fight but they could hear what
it was about and that's the way things were and stayed
and are except that in time the sounds started to
sound different (familiarity) and that was English

                         well, that Past we have always with us, eh?
                         I am talking about the color of money
                         the dime so red and the 100 dollar bill so orchid
                         the sickly fuchsia of a 1 the optimistic
                         orange of a 5 the useless penny like a seed
                         the magnificent yellow zinnia of a 10
                         especially a roll of them the airy blue of a
                         50 how pretty a house is when it's filled with them
                         that's not a villa that's a bank
                         where's the ocean
now this is not a tract against usury it's just putting two and two together
                                    and getting five (thank you, Mae)

      actually I want to hear more about your family
                                    yes you get the beer

I am actually thinking about how much I love Lena Horne
I never intended to go to New Hampshire without you
you know there's an interesting divinity in Rarotonga that looks sort of like you

"I am a woman in love" he said
the day began with the clear blue sky and ended in the Parrot Garden
the day began and ended with my finding you in the Parrot Garden
Lena Horne had vanished into a taxi and we were moreorless alone together
of course it wasn't Lena Horne it was Simone Signoret we were happy anyway

"As if a clear lake meddling with itself
Should cloud its pureness with a muddy gloom"

"My steeds are all pawing at the threshold of the morn"

favorites: going to parties with you, being in corners at parties with you,
being in gloomy pubs with you smiling, poking you at parties when
you're "down," coming on like South Pacific with you at them,
shrimping with you into the Russian dressing, leaving parties with
you alone to go and eat a piece of cloud

YIPE! 504 nails in *The Gross Clinic!*
it's more interesting to see a Princess dance
with a Bluebird than just two bluebirds
dancing through diagonal vista together

at the flea circus there was a bargain-hunter
at the end of the road a bum, the blue year
commenced with an enormous sale of loneliness
and everyone came back with a little something
one a baby, one a tooth, one a case of clap
and, best of all, a friend bought a medical dispensary
there were a lot of limbs lying around so
of course someone created a ballet company, oke
the barely possible snow sifted into a solid crystal
I sometimes think you are Mozart's nephew: "Talk
to me Harry Winston, tell me all about it!"

"from August to October
the sun drips down the sign

for eating at midnight ask Virgo
to be lost outside the cafeteria"

I went to Albania for coffee and came back for the rent day
"I think somebody oughta go through your mind with a good eraser"
meanwhile Joe is tracing love and hate back to the La Brea tar-pits

hear that rattling?
those aren't marbles in my head they're chains on my ankles

why do you say you're a bottle and you feed me
the sky is more blue and it is getting cold
last night I saw Garfinkel's Surgical Supply truck
and knew I was near "home" though dazed and thoughtful
what did you do to make me think
after we led the bum to the hospital
and you got into the cab
I was feeling lost myself

(ALWAYS)

never to lose those moments in the Carlyle without a tie

endless as a stick-pin barely visible you
drown whatever one thought of as perception and
let all the clouds in under the yellow heaters
meeting   somewhere over St. Louis
call me earlier because I might want to do something else
except eat   ugh

endlessly unraveling itself before the Christopher Columbus Tavern
quite a series was born   as where I am going is to
Quo Vadis for lunch
out there in the blabbing wind and glass   c'est l'azur

perhaps
marinated duck saddle with foot sauce and a tumbler of vodka
picking at my fevered brain
perhaps
letting you off the hook at last or leaning on you in the theatre

oh plankton!
"mes poèmes lyriques, à partir de 1897, peuvent se lire comme un journal intime"

yes always though you said it first
you the quicksand and sand and grass
as I wave toward you freely
the ego–ridden sea
there is a light there that neither
of us will obscure
rubbing it all white
saving ships from fucking up on the rocks
on the infinite waves of skin smelly and crushed and light and absorbed

1962

POEM

Lana Turner has collapsed!
I was trotting along and suddenly
it started raining and snowing
and you said it was hailing
but hailing hits you on the head
hard so it was really snowing and
raining and I was in such a hurry
to meet you but the traffic
was acting exactly like the sky
and suddenly I see a headline
LANA TURNER HAS COLLAPSED!
there is no snow in Hollywood
there is no rain in California
I have been to lots of parties
and acted perfectly disgraceful
but I never actually collapsed
oh Lana Turner we love you get up

1962

FIRST DANCES

I

From behind he takes her waist
and lifts her, her lavender waist
stained with tears and her mascara
is running, her neck is tired
from drooping. She floats she steps
automatically correct, then suddenly
she is alive up there and smiles.
How much greater triumph for him
that she had so despaired when his
hands encircled her like a pillar
and lifted her into the air
which after him will turn to rock-
like boredom, but not till after
many hims and he will not be there.

2

The punch bowl was near the cloakroom
so the pints could be taken out of the
boys' cloaks and dumped into the punch.
Outside the branches beat hysterically
towards the chandeliers, just fended
off by fearful windows. The chandeliers
giggle a little. There were many
introductions but few invitations. I
found a spot of paint on my coat as
others found pimples. It is easy to
dance it is even easy to dance together
sometimes. We were very young and ugly
we knew it, everybody knew it.

3

A white hall inside a church. Nerves.

1962

ANSWER TO VOZNESENSKY & EVTUSHENKO

We are tired of your tiresome imitations of Mayakovsky
we are tired
        of your dreary tourist ideas of our Negro selves
our selves are in far worse condition than the obviousness
of your color sense
        your general sense of Poughkeepsie is
a gaucherie no American poet would be guilty of in Tiflis
thanks to French Impressionism
        we do not pretend to know more
than can be known
        how many sheets have you stained with your semen
oh Tartars, and how many
        of our loves have you illuminated with
your heart your breath
        as we poets of America have loved you
your countrymen, our countrymen, our lives, your lives, and
the dreary expanses of your translations
        your idiotic manifestos
and the strange black cock which has become ours despite your envy

we do what we feel
        you do not even do what you must or can
I do not love you any more since Mayakovsky died and Pasternak
theirs was the death of my nostalgia for your tired ignorant race
since you insist on race
        you shall not take my friends away from me
because they live in Harlem
        you shall not make Mississippi into Sakhalin
you came too late, a lovely talent doesn't make a ball
    I consider myself to be black and you not even part
where you see death
        you see a dance of death
            which is
imperialist, implies training, requires techniques
our ballet does not employ
        you are indeed as cold as wax
as your progenitor was red, and how greatly we loved his redness

in the fullness of our own idiotic sun! what
"roaring universe" outshouts his violent triumphant sun!
        you are not even speaking
                          in a whisper
     Mayakovsky's hat worn by a horse

1963

AGAIN, JOHN KEATS, OR THE POT OF BASIL

Just when I was getting completely through
dried out, balled up, anxious and empty
like a gulch in a John Huston movie
I went to see *Strange Interlude* and began
to go away for a weekend on the beach
into that theatre again and again
now I have a pot of basil a friend gave
me and am reading Keats again and realize
that everything is impossible in a different way
well so what, but there's a difference
between a window and a wall again

1963

[THE LIGHT PRESSES DOWN]

The light presses down
in an empty head the trees
and bushes flop like
a little girl imitating
The Dying Swan the stone
is hot the church is a
Russian oven and we
are traveling still

you come by to type
your poems and write a
new poem instead on my
old typewriter while I sit
and read a novel about
a lunatic's analysis of
a poem by Robert Frost
it is all suffocating

I am still traveling
with Belinda Lee where
does she take me Africa
where it is hot enough
even to make the elephant
angry and the grass is
all withered and TV color

why do I always read
Russian exile novels in
summer I guess because
they're full of snow
and it is good to cry a
little to match your sweat
and sweat a little
to match their tears

1963

WALKING

I get a cinder in my eye
                    it streams into
        the sunlight
                    the air pushes it aside
and I drop my hot dog
                    into one of the Seagram Building's
fountains
            it is all watery and clear and windy

the shape of the toe as
                    it describes the pain
of the ball of the foot,
                    walking walking on
asphalt
        the strange embrace of the ankle's
lock
        on the pavement
                    squared like mausoleums
but cheerful
            moved over and stamped on
slapped by winds
                the country is no good for us
there's nothing
            to bump into
                        or fall apart glassily
there's not enough
                poured concrete
                            and brassy
reflections
        the wind now takes me to
The Narrows
        and I see it rising there
                        New York
greater than the Rocky Mountains

1964

POEM

for Mario Schifano

I to you and you to me the endless oceans of
                              dilapidated crossing
everybody up
                  the stench of whoopee steerage and candy
                                          cane, for
never the cool free call of the brink
                              but cut it out this
is getting to be another poem about Hart Crane

                                          do you find
the hot dogs better here than at
                              Rosati's, the pepper mills
lousier, the butter softer
                          the acrid dryness of your paper
already reminded me of
                      New York's sky in August before the
nasal rains
                  the soot comes down in a nice umber for the scalp

and when the cartoon
                  of a pietà
                              begins to resemble Ava Gardner
in Mexico
            you know you're here
                              welcome to the bull ring
and Chicago and the mush in the enclosures
                                      so brave

    so free so blind

                      where the drawings are produced on skin, not
forever
          to stay under

it's not the end

                        but for tattoos, you will

like it here, being away and walking

                      turning it into sky again

1964

FANTASY

(dedicated to the health of Allen Ginsberg)

How do you like the music of Adolph

                Deutsch? I like
it, I like it better than Max Steiner's. Take his
score for *Northern Pursuit,* the Helmut Dantine theme
was . . .

          and then the window fell on my hand. Errol
Flynn was skiing by. Down

                  down down went the grim
grey submarine under the "cold" ice.

                    Helmut was
safely ashore, on the ice.

              What dreams, what incredible
fantasies of snow farts will this all lead to?

                      I
don't know, I have stopped thinking like a sled dog.

The main thing is to tell a story.

              It is almost
very important. Imagine

              throwing away the avalanche
so early in the movie. I am the only spy left
in Canada,

        but just because I'm alone in the snow
doesn't necessarily mean I'm a Nazi.

              Let's see,
two aspirins a vitamin C tablet and some baking soda
should do the trick, that's practically an

              Alka
Seltzer. Allen come out of the bathroom

                and take it.
I think someone put butter on my skis instead
of wax.

        Ouch. The leanto is falling over in the
firs, and there is another fatter spy here. They
didn't tell me they sent

            him. Well, that takes care

of him, boy were those huskies hungry.

                              Allen,
are you feeling any better? Yes, I'm crazy about
Helmut Dantine

                    but I'm glad that Canada will remain
free. Just free, that's all, never argue with the movies.

                                        1964

CANTATA

How could I be so foolish as to not believe
that my great orange cat Boris *(Armed with Madness)*
Butts loves me when he runs to the door like a dog
each night when I come home from work and
probably isn't even particularly hungry
                                        or lays
his conspicuous hairs on my darkest clothes
out of pure longing for my smell which they do have
because he looks like my best friend my constant lover
hopelessly loyal tawny and apt and whom I hopelessly love

1965

LITTLE ELEGY FOR ANTONIO MACHADO

Now your protesting demons summon themselves
    with fire against the Castilian dark
and solitary light
        your mother dead on the hearth
and your heart at rest on the border of constellary futures

no domesticated cemeteries can enshroud your flight
    of linear solarities and quiescent tumbrils
vision of the carrion
        past made glassy and golden
to reveal the dark, the dark in all its ancestral clarity

where our futures lie increasingly in fire
    twisted ropes of sound encrusting our brains
your water air and earth
        insist on our joining you
in recognition of colder prides and less negotiable ambitions

we shall continue to correct all classical revisions
    of ourselves as trials of ceremonial worth
and purple excess
        improving your soul's expansion
in the night and developing our own in salt-like praise

1966

PERSONISM: A MANIFESTO

Everything is in the poems, but at the risk of sounding like the poor wealthy man's Allen Ginsberg I will write to you because I just heard that one of my fellow poets thinks that a poem of mine that can't be got at one reading is because I was confused too. Now, come on. I don't believe in god, so I don't have to make elaborately sounded structures. I hate Vachel Lindsay, always have; I don't even like rhythm, assonance, all that stuff. You just go on your nerve. If someone's chasing you down the street with a knife you just run, you don't turn around and shout, "Give it up! I was a track star for Mineola Prep."

That's for the writing poems part. As for their reception, suppose you're in love and someone's mistreating *(mal aimé)* you, you don't say, "Hey, you can't hurt me this way, I care!" you just let all the different bodies fall where they may, and they always do may after a few months. But that's not why you fell in love in the first place, just to hang onto life, so you have to take your chances and try to avoid being logical. Pain always produces logic, which is very bad for you.

I'm not saying that I don't have practically the most lofty ideas of anyone writing today, but what difference does that make? They're just ideas. The only good thing about it is that when I get lofty enough I've stopped thinking and that's when refreshment arrives.

But how can you really care if anybody gets it, or gets what it means, or if it improves them. Improves them for what? For death? Why hurry them along? Too many poets act like a middle-aged mother trying to get her kids to eat too much cooked meat, and potatoes with drippings (tears). I don't give a damn whether they eat or not. Forced feeding leads to excessive thinness (effete). Nobody should experience anything they don't need to, if they don't need poetry bully for them. I like the movies too. And after all, only Whitman and Crane and Williams, of the American poets, are better than the movies. As for measure and other technical apparatus, that's just common sense: if you're going to buy a pair of pants you want them to be tight enough so everyone will want to go to bed with you. There's nothing metaphysical about it. Unless, of course, you flatter yourself into thinking that what you're experiencing is "yearning."

Abstraction in poetry, which Allen [Ginsberg] recently commented on in *It Is*, is intriguing. I think it appears mostly in the minute particulars where decision is necessary. Abstraction (in poetry, not in painting) involves personal removal by the poet. For instance, the decision involved in the choice between "the nostalgia *of* the infinite" and "the nostalgia *for* the infinite" defines an attitude towards degree of abstraction. The nostalgia *of* the infinite representing the greater degree of abstraction, removal, and negative capability (as in Keats and Mallarmé). Personism, a movement which I recently founded and which nobody knows about, interests me a great deal, being so totally opposed to this kind of abstract removal that it is verging on a true abstraction for the first time, really, in the history of poetry. Personism is to Wallace Stevens what *la poésie pure* was to Béranger. Personism has nothing to do with philosophy, it's all art. It does not have to do with personality or intimacy, far from it! But to give you a vague idea, one of its minimal aspects is to address itself to one person (other than the poet himself), thus evoking overtones of love without destroying love's life-giving vulgarity, and sustaining the poet's feelings towards the poem while preventing love from distracting him into feeling about the person. That's part of Personism. It was founded by me after lunch with LeRoi Jones on August 27, 1959, a day in which I was in love with someone (not Roi, by the way, a blond). I went back to work and wrote a poem for this person. While I was writing it I was realizing that if I wanted to I could use the telephone instead of writing the poem, and so Personism was born. It's a very exciting movement which will undoubtedly have lots of adherents. It puts the poem squarely between the poet and the person, Lucky Pierre style, and the poem is correspondingly gratified. The poem is at last between two persons instead of two pages. In all modesty, I confess that it may be the death of literature as we know it. While I have certain regrets, I am still glad I got there before Alain Robbe-Grillet did. Poetry being quicker and surer than prose, it is only just that poetry finish literature off. For a time people thought that Artaud was going to accomplish this, but actually, for all their magnificence, his polemical writings are not more outside literature than Bear Mountain is outside New York State. His relation is no more astounding than Dubuffet's to painting.

What can we expect of Personism? (This is getting good, isn't it?) Everything, but we won't get it. It is too new, too vital a movement to promise anything. But it, like Africa, is on the way. The recent propagandists for technique on the one hand, and for content on the other, had better watch out.

1959

[STATEMENT FOR *THE NEW AMERICAN POETRY*]

I am mainly preoccupied with the world as I experience it, and at times when I would rather be dead the thought that I could never write another poem has so far stopped me. I think this is an ignoble attitude. I would rather die for love, but I haven't.

I don't think of fame or posterity (as Keats so grandly and genuinely did), nor do I care about clarifying experiences for anyone or bettering (other than accidentally) anyone's state or social relation, nor am I for any particular technical development in the American language simply because I find it necessary. What is happening to me, allowing for lies and exaggerations which I try to avoid, goes into my poems. I don't think my experiences are clarified or made beautiful for myself or anyone else; they are just there in whatever form I can find them. What is clear to me in my work is probably obscure to others, and vice versa. My formal "stance" is found at the crossroads where what I know and can't get meets what is left of that I know and can bear without hatred. I dislike a great deal of contemporary poetry—all of the past you read is usually quite great—but it is a useful thorn to have in one's side.

It may be that poetry makes life's nebulous events tangible to me and restores their detail; or conversely, that poetry brings forth the intangible quality of incidents which are all too concrete and circumstantial. Or each on specific occasions, or both all the time.

1959

It is very difficult for me to write a statement for Paterson, much as I would find it agreeable to do so if I could. So perhaps it could take the form of a letter? and not be a real statement. Because if I did write a statement it would probably be so non-pertinent to anything you might want to know in connection with my actual poems. The only two starts I have been able to think of since you first asked me for one, are (1) to begin with a description of what I would like my poetry to be, or hope it is (already? in the future? I don't know). This would be a description of the effect other things have had upon me which I in my more day-dreamy moments wish that I could effect in others. Well you can't have a statement saying "My poetry is the Sistine Chapel of verse," or "My poetry is just like Pollock, de Kooning and Guston rolled into one great verb," or "My poetry is like a windy day on a hill overlooking the stormy ocean"—first of all it isn't so far as I can tell, and secondly even if it were something like all of these that wouldn't be because I managed to make it that way. I couldn't, it must have been an accident, and I would probably not recognize it myself. Further, what would poetry like that be? It would have to be the Sistine Chapel itself, the paintings themselves, the day and time specifically. Impossible.

Or (2) if I then abandoned that idea and wrote you about my convictions concerning form, measure, sound, yardage, placement and ear—well, if I went into that thoroughly enough nobody would ever want to read the poems I've already written, they would have been so thoroughly described, and I would have to do everything the opposite in the future to avoid my own boredom, and where would I be? That's where I am anyway, I suppose, but at least this way it's not self-induced. Besides, I can't think of any more than one poem at a time, so I would end up with a "poetics" based on one of my poems which any other poem of mine would completely contradict except for certain affections or habits of speech they might include. So that would be of no use for general readers, and misleading for anyone who had already read any of my poems. So, as they say in the Café Flore, it's better to *tas gueule*. I'm not giving up responsibility for the poems. I definitely don't believe that "your idea is as good as anyone's about what it means." But I don't want to make up a lot of prose about something that is perfectly clear in the poems. If you cover someone with earth and grass grows, you don't know what they looked like any more. Critical prose makes too much grass grow, and I don't want to help hide my own poems, much less kill them.

I know you will think of the remarks I made for Don Allen's anthology and that "Manifesto" in LeRoi Jones's *Yūgen*. In the case of the manifesto I think it was all right because it was a little diary of my thoughts, after lunch with LeRoi walking back to work, about the poem I turned out to be just about to write ("Personal Poem," which he published in an earlier issue of *Yūgen*). It was, as a matter of fact, intended for Don Allen's anthology, and I was encouraged to write it because LeRoi told me at lunch that he had written a statement for the anthology. But Don Allen thought it unwise to use it in relation to the earlier poems included, quite rightly, so I wrote another which he did use. This latter, it seems to me now, is even more mistaken, pompous, and quite untrue, as compared to the manifesto. But it is also, like the manifesto, a diary of a particular day and the depressed mood of that day (it's a pretty depressing day, you must admit, when you feel you relate more importantly to poetry than to life), and as such may perhaps have more general application to my poetry since I have been more often depressed than happy, as far as I can tally it up. In the case of either, it's a hopeless conundrum: it used to be that I could only write when I was miserable; now I can only write when I'm happy. Where will it all end? At any rate, this will explain why I can't really say anything definite for the Paterson Society for the time being.

1961

V. R. LANG: A MEMOIR

I first saw Bunny Lang 10 years ago at a cocktail party in a book store in Cambridge, Massachusetts. She was sitting in a corner sulking and biting her lower lip—long blonde hair, brown eyes, Roman-striped skirt. As if it were a movie, she was glamorous and aloof. The girl I was talking to said: "That's Bunny Lang. I'd like to give her a good slap."

We met a few weeks later and began a friendship which was unique—in my life, at least; perhaps not in hers, for she always kept certain areas of mystery intact. We had a fencing period: we sounded each other out for hours over beers, talking incessantly. We were both young poets and poetry was our major concern.

We both loved Rimbaud and Auden; she thought I loved Rimbaud too much, and I thought the same about Auden and her. She simply couldn't like Cocteau and couldn't bear *Ivan the Terrible*. "It's so black," she would say, "I don't believe a minute of it!" And we then began our "coffee talks" which were to go on for years, sometimes long distance. At 11 each morning we called each other and discussed everything we had thought of since we had parted the night before, including any dreams we may have had in the meantime. And once we were going to write a modern Coffee Cantata together, but never did.

She worked on her poems and plays in secrecy, withdrawn in the big room at the top of the old Boston house, looking out at the Charles River and ignoring her two noisy Siamese cats, which were almost always in heat. She would type her poems over and over, sometimes 40 times, sinking into them and understanding them. As for the theatre, she loved to sing, act, and dance, all of which she did with extraordinary charm and wit. Her first ideas for the theatre were on the charade or satire level; it was not until she began working on her first long play, *Fire Exit*, that her characteristic poetic process moved onstage, and in *Arcadia* it has found its starring role, a pastoral played in depth of feeling and solitude. A modern "Shepheards Calendar," the lovers rehearse for each other the seasons and the years, tarnished lovers seeking a justification for existence in their love. There on their island the City presses down upon them, initiating the failure of love, which is death.

Bunny's poems are full of the many things she did, the trips, the adventures, the stint with the Canadian WAC during the war, the literati in the *Chicago Review* days, the avant-garde in the Village, the circus on the stage, and through them all runs the strong line of her private world, the personal gaiety and suffering which relates her experiences and forms her existence. In *I Too Have Lived in Arcadia* appears the ultimate expression of her experience, and in these days of overnaturalism in the theatre, it is good to have a work for the theatre which is poetry, which articulately faces the hip compulsive with the pterodactyl and ponders both the survival of the fittest and the fitness of the survivor.

> Perhaps we have become like cave creatures,
> Who, being blind, can only the blind beget.
> Sight is becoming useless. We are turning black. Well,
> We will sweat now, like shuddering mountains
> Struggling to grow in the millions of long time.
> But squashed in the heart of us, surely there are footsteps
> Of all the monsters who kept us alive.

In the summer of 1956, V. R. Lang died at the age of 32, the courage and fastidiousness of her life matched only by that of her work. And gradually that clear image of herself which is her work will be the sole image, a beautiful image, faithful to the original.

1957

A PERSONAL PREFACE

I am sitting here and cool sunlight, pretending to be warm, is coming through the window. Near me is a small color photograph of Bunny Lang, blonde, dark-eyed, ironically smiling, and in front of me a little toy tiger she once gave me, with a red ribbon around its waist. On the radio *Wozzeck* is playing, a work we often argued lovingly about (where Bunny didn't at first accept all the music, she was crazy about the heroine, Marie).

I also have a black dunce-cap, decorated with silver bells. She gave it to me to wear when I wrote. "It will keep you relaxed," she said, "free from distractions. It will keep away SPOOKS!" When Bunny was your friend, she was not only a dear friend, she was also the guardian of that friendship. And the guardian of so much else besides! of her own mysterious dreams, her strange insights, her sometimes savage honesty. You see this in the heroines of her plays who, like Marie, are beset but unyielding.

It is now five years since she died; it seems a moment, it seems it didn't happen at all. She is calling us long distance in these poems, telling us how it is with her, how bright things can be, how terrible things are. She was a wonderful person. She is one of our finest poets. We are so lucky to have something of her still!

1961

LARRY RIVERS: A MEMOIR

I first met Larry Rivers in 1950. When I first started coming down to New York from Harvard for weekends Larry was in Europe and friends had said we would like each other. Finally, at for me a very literary cocktail party at John Ashbery's we did meet, and we did like each other: I thought he was crazy and he thought I was even crazier. I was very shy, which he thought was intelligence; he was garrulous, which I assumed was brilliance—and on such misinterpretations, thank heavens, many a friendship is based. On the other hand, perhaps it was not a misinterpretation: certain of my literary "heroes" of the *Partisan Review* variety present at that party paled in significance when I met Larry, and through these years have remained pale while Larry has been something of a hero to me, which would seem to make me intelligent and Larry brilliant. Who knows?

The milieu of those days, and it's funny to think of them in such a way since they are so recent, seems odd now. We were all in our early twenties. John Ashbery, Barbara Guest, Kenneth Koch and I, being poets, divided our time between the literary bar, the San Remo, and the artists' bar, the Cedar Tavern. In the San Remo we argued and gossiped: in the Cedar we often wrote poems while listening to the painters argue and gossip. So far as I know nobody painted in the San Remo while they listened to the writers argue. An interesting sidelight to these social activities was that for most of us non-academic and indeed non-literary poets in the sense of the American scene at the time, the painters were the only generous audience for our poetry, and most of us read first publicly in art galleries or at The Club. The literary establishment cared about as much for our work as the Frick cared for Pollock and de Kooning, not that we cared any more about establishments than they did, all of the disinterested parties being honorable men.

Then there was great respect for anyone who did anything marvelous: when Larry introduced me to de Kooning I nearly got sick, as I almost did when I met Auden; if Jackson Pollock tore the door off the men's room in the Cedar it was something he just did and was interesting, not an annoyance. You couldn't see into it anyway, and besides there was then a sense of genius. Or what Kline used to call "the dream." Newman was at that time considered a temporarily silent oracle, being ill, Ad Reinhardt the most shrewd critic of the emergent "art world," Meyer Schapiro a god and Alfred Barr right up there alongside him but more distant, Holger Cahill another god but one who had abdicated to become more interested in "the thing we're doing," Clement Greenberg the discoverer, Harold Rosenberg the analyzer, and so on and so on. Tom Hess had written the important book. Elaine de Kooning was the White Goddess: she knew everything, told little of it though she talked a lot, and we all adored (and adore) her. She is graceful.

Into this scene Larry came rather like a demented telephone. Nobody knew whether they wanted it in the library, the kitchen or the toilet, but it was electric. Nor did he. The single most important event in his artistic career was when de Kooning said his painting was like pressing your face into wet grass. From the whole jazz scene, which had gradually diminished to a mere recreation, Larry had emerged into the world of art with the sanction of one of his own gods, and indeed the only living one.

It is interesting to think of 1950–52, and the styles of a whole group of young artists whom I knew rather intimately. It was a liberal education on top of an academic one. Larry was chiefly involved with Bonnard and Renoir at first, later Manet and Soutine; Joan Mitchell—Duchamp; Mike Goldberg—Cézanne–Villon–de Kooning; Helen Frankenthaler—Pollock-Miró; Al Leslie—Motherwell; De Niro—Matisse; Nell Blaine—Helion; Hartigan—Pollock-Guston; Harry Jackson—a lot of Matisse with a little German Expressionism; Jane Freilicher—a more subtle combination of Soutine with some Monticelli and Moreau appearing through the paint. The impact of THE NEW AMERICAN PAINTING on this group was being avoided rather self-consciously rather than exploited. If you live in the studio next to Brancusi, you try to think about Poussin. If you drink with Kline you tend to do your black-and-whites in pencil on paper. The artists I knew at that time knew perfectly well who was Great and they weren't going to begin to imitate their works, only their spirit. When someone did a false Clyfford Still or Rothko, it was talked about for weeks. They hadn't read Sartre's *Being and Nothingness* for nothing.

Larry was especially interested in the vast range of possibilities of art. Perhaps because of his experience as a jazz musician, where everything can become fixed so quickly in style and become "the sound," he has moved restlessly from phase to phase. Larry always wanted to see something when he painted, unlike the then-prevalent conceptualized approach. No matter what stylistic period he was in, the friends he spent most time with were invariably subjects in some sense, more or less recognizable, and of course his two sons and his mother-in-law who lived with him were the most frequent subjects (he was separated from his wife, Augusta). His mother-in-law, Mrs. Bertha Burger, was the most frequent subject. She was called Berdie by everyone, a woman of infinite patience and sweetness, who held together a Bohemian household of such staggering complexity it would have driven a less great woman mad. She had a natural grace of temperament which overcame all obstacles and irritations. (During her fatal illness she confessed to me that she had once actually disliked two of Larry's friends because they had been "mean" to her grandsons, and this apologetically!) She appears in every period: an early Soutinesque painting with a cat; at an Impressionistic breakfast table; in the semi-abstract paintings of her seated in a wicker chair; as the double nude, very realistic, now in the collection of the Whitney Museum; in the later *The Athlete's Dream,* which she especially enjoyed because I posed with her and it made her less self-conscious if she was in a painting with a friend; she is also all the figures in the Museum of Modern Art's great painting *The Pool*. Her gentle interestedness extended beyond her own family to everyone who frequented the house, in a completely incurious way. Surrounded by painters and poets suddenly in mid-life, she had an admirable directness with esthetic decisions: "it must be very good work, he's such a wonderful person." Considering the polemics of the time, this was not only a relaxing attitude, it was an adorable one. For many of us her death was as much the personal end of a period as Pollock's death was that of a public one.

I mention these details of Rivers' life because, in the sense that Picasso meant it, his work is very much a diary of his experience. He is inspired directly by visual stimulation and his work is ambitious to save these experiences. Where much of the art of our time has been involved with direct conceptual or ethical considerations, Rivers has chosen to mirror his preoccupations and enthusiasms in an unprogrammatic way. As an example, I think that he personally was very awed by Rothko and that this reveals itself in the seated figures of 1953–54; at the same time I know that a rereading of *War and Peace*, and his idea of Tolstoy's life, prompted him to commence work on *Washington Crossing the Delaware*, a non-historical, non-philosophical work, the impulse for which I at first thought was hopelessly corny until I saw the painting finished. Rivers veers sharply, as if totally dependent on life impulses, until one observes an obsessively willful insistence on precisely what he is interested in. This goes for the father of our country as well as for the later Camel and Tareyton packs. Who, he seems to be saying, says they're corny? This is the opposite of pop art. He is never naive and never oversophisticated.

Less known than his jazz interests are Larry's literary ones. He has kept, sporadically, a fairly voluminous and definitely scandalous journal, has written some good poems of a diaristic (boosted by Surrealism) nature, and collaborated with several poets (including myself) who have posed for him, mainly I think to keep them quiet while posing and to relax himself when not painting or sculpting. The literary side of his activity has resulted mainly in the poem-paintings with Kenneth Koch, a series of lithographs with me *[Stones]*, and our great collaborative play *Kenneth Koch, a Tragedy*, which cannot be printed because it is so filled with 50s art gossip that everyone would sue us. This latter work kept me amused enough to continue to pose for the big nude which took so many months to finish. That is one of Larry's strategies to keep you coming back to his studio, or was when he couldn't afford a professional model. The separation of the arts, in the "pure" sense, has never interested him. As early as 1952, when John Myers and Herbert Machiz were producing the New York Artists' Theatre, Larry did a set for a play of mine, *Try! Try!* At the first run-through I realized it was all wrong and withdrew it. He, however, insisted that if he had done the work for the set I should be willing to rewrite to my own satisfaction, and so I rewrote the play for Anne Meacham, J. D. Cannon, Louis Edmonds and Larry's set, and that is the version printed by Grove Press. Few people are so generous towards the work of others.

As I said earlier, Larry is restless, impulsive and compulsive. He loves to work. I remember a typical moment in the late 50s when both Joan Mitchell and I were visiting the Hamptons and we were all lying on the beach, a state of relaxation Larry can never tolerate for long. Joan was wearing a particularly attractive boating hat and Larry insisted that they go back to his studio so he could make a drawing of her. It is a beautiful drawing, an interesting moment in their lives, and Joan was not only pleased to be drawn, she was relieved because she is terribly vulnerable to sunburn. As Kenneth Koch once said of him, "Larry has a floating subconscious—he's all intuition and no sense."

That's an interesting observation about the person, but actually Larry Rivers brings such a barrage of technical gifts to each intuitive occasion that the moment is totally transformed. Many of these gifts were acquired in the same manner as his talents in music and literature, through practice. Having been hired by Herbie Fields' band in his teens he became adept at the saxophone, meeting a group of poets who interested him he absorbed, pro or con, lots of ideas about style in poetry, and attending classes at Hans Hofmann's school plunged him into activities which were to make him one of the best draftsmen in contemporary art and one of the most subtle and particular colorists. This has been accomplished through work rather than intellection. And here an analogy to jazz can be justified: his hundreds of drawings are each like a separate performance, with its own occasion and subject, and what has been "learned" from the performance is not just the technical facility of the classical pianists' octaves or the studies in a *Grande Chaumière* class, but the ability to deal with the increased skills that deepening of subject matter and the risks of anxiety-dictated variety demand for clear expression. Where Rivers draws a nose, it is my nose, your nose, his nose, Gogol's nose, and the nose from a drawing instruction manual, and it is the result of highly conscious skill.

There is a little bit of Hemingway in his attitude toward ability, toward what you do to a canvas or an armature. His early painting, *The Burial,* is really, in a less arrogant manner than Hemingway's, "getting into the ring" with Courbet *(A Burial at Ornans),* just as his nude portrait of me started in his mind from envy of the then newly acquired Géricault slave with the rope at the Metropolitan Museum, the portrait *Augusta* from a Delacroix; and even this year he is still fighting it out, this time with David's *Napoleon.* As with his friends, as with cigarette and cigar boxes, maps, and animals, he is always engaged in an esthetic athleticism which sharpens the eye, hand and arm in order to beat the bugaboos of banality and boredom, deliberately invited into the painting and then triumphed over.

What his work has always had to say to me, I guess, is to be more keenly interested while I'm still alive. And perhaps this is the most important thing art can say.

1965

Short Chronology

1926   Born in Baltimore, Maryland, on March 27. Birthday celebrated on June 27.

1927–44   Family returned to Grafton, Massachusetts. Attended parochial schools in Worcester. Studied piano privately from an early age and later studied piano and harmony at the New England Conservatory of Music.

1944–46   Served during World War II as a sonarman on the U.S.S. *Nicholas*. Stationed at Norfolk, Virginia; San Francisco, California; the South Pacific and Japan.

1946–50   Received a BA in English at Harvard College. Studied poetry with John Ciardi. Published poems and stories in *The Harvard Advocate*. Participated in founding the Poets' Theatre. Met John Ashbery, Hal Fondren, Ted Gorey, Violet (Bunny) Lang, George Montgomery, and Larry Osgood. When he visited New York, met Jane Freilicher, Kenneth Koch, Fairfield Porter, and Larry Rivers.

1950–51   Received a MA in English at the University of Michigan, Ann Arbor. Received a major Hopwood Award in Creative Writing for *A Byzantine Place: 50 Poems and a Noh Play* (1951). *Try! Try!* and *Change Your Bedding* produced by the Poets' Theatre (1951). Composed music for John Ashbery's *Everyman*. Moved to 326 East 49th Street in New York. Met James Schuyler and Joseph LeSueur. Began front-desk work at the Museum of Modern Art.

1952   *A City Winter and Other Poems* published by the Tibor de Nagy Gallery. Met Edwin Denby, Helen Frankenthaler, Michael Goldberg, Barbara Guest, Philip Guston, Grace Hartigan, Franz Kline, Elaine and Willem de Kooning, Alfred Leslie, Joan Mitchell, Jackson Pollock, and Ned Rorem. Participated in several panel discussions at the Club of the New York Painters on 8th Street.

1953–5   *Oranges: 12 Pastorals* published by the Tibor de Nagy Gallery for the exhibit of Grace Hartigan's *Oranges*. "Nature and New American Painting" published in *Folder 3*. Left the museum and became an editorial associate of *ARTNews*. Contributed short reviews and articles. Second version of *Try! Try!* produced by the Artists' Theatre.

1955–66 Rejoined the Museum of Modern Art in 1955 as a special assistant in the International Program. Assisted in the organization of important traveling exhibitions, including *The New American Painting* circulated in Europe 1958–59, and *Twentieth Century Italian Art from American Collections* (Milan and Rome, 1960). Appointed assistant curator of painting and sculpture exhibitions in 1960; appointed associate curator in 1965. Selected U.S. representations for the following international exhibitions: IV International Art Exhibition, Japan, 1957; IV Bienal, São Paulo, Brazil, 1957 (selections comprising a group exhibition of five painters and three sculptors and *Jackson Pollock: 1912–56*, a memorial exhibition that later traveled in Europe, 1958–59); XXIX Venice Biennale, 1958 (Seymour Lipton and Mark Tobey sections); with Porter A. McCray, *Documenta II '59*, Kassel, Germany, 1959; and VI Bienal, 1961, São Paulo, Brazil (Robert Motherwell and Reuben Nakian sections). The following exhibitions were shown at the Museum of Modern Art: *New Spanish Painting and Sculpture*, 1960; *Robert Motherwell*, 1965; and *Reuben Nakian*, 1966. Other exhibitions under his direction which traveled widely after 1961 include: *Magritte-Tanguy*; *Abstract Watercolors by 14 Americans*; *Gaston Lachaise*; *Drawings by Arshile Gorky*; *Drawings by David Smith*; *Franz Kline*; *Recent Landscapes by 8 Americans*; *Robert Motherwell*; *Works on Paper*; and *David Smith*. With René d'Harnoncourt, director of the museum, co-directed *Modern Sculpture: U.S.A.* (Paris, Berlin, and Baden-Baden, 1965–66). At the time of his death, had started work as curator for a Jackson Pollock retrospective.

1956 Received a one-semester fellowship at the Poets' Theatre in Cambridge, where he produced and acted in John Ashbery's *The Compromise*. Met John Wieners. Collaborated with Arnold Weinstein and John Gruen on the musical comedy *The Undercover Lover*. Met Norman Bluhm.

1957 Moved to 90 University Place. *Meditations in an Emergency* published by Grove Press. Met Gregory Corso, Allen Ginsberg, and Jack Kerouac. From 1957–59 collaborated with Larry Rivers on *Stones*, thirteen lithographs published in 1959 by Universal Limited Art Editions.

1958 "Franz Kline Talking" published in *Evergreen Review*. Met Kynaston McShine and Alex Katz. First trip to Europe, where he met many Spanish artists who were later included in the *New Spanish Painting and Sculpture* exhibition; visited Berlin, Venice Biennale, Rome, and Paris. Met Patsy Southgate.

1959 Moved to 441 East Ninth Street. *Jackson Pollock* published by George Braziller. "About Zhivago and His Poems" published in *Evergreen Review*. "An

Interview with Larry Rivers" published in *Horizon*. *Love's Labor, an eclogue* produced by the Living Theater. Met the dancer Vincent Warren, LeRoi Jones, Bill Berkson, Frank Lima, Tony Towle, and other young poets.

1960   *Odes*, with five serigraphs by Mike Goldberg, published by Tiber Press. *Second Avenue* published by Totem/Corinth Press. Curated exhibition and wrote catalog essay for *New Spanish Painting and Sculpture* at the Museum of Modern Art. "Awake in Spain" produced by the Living Theater and published in *Hasty Papers. Try! Try!* included in *Artists' Theatre*, edited by Herbert Machiz, published by Grove Press. Collaborated on twenty-six poem-paintings with Norman Bluhm. Met J. J. Mitchell. Traveled to Spain to organize the exhibition of Spanish painting and sculpture, then to Paris.

1961–62   Became editor of the quarterly *Kulchur* and contributed "Art Chronicles" and other essays. Met David Shapiro. Received a grant from the Merrill Foundation (1962) and took a brief leave from the museum to write.

1963–64   Taught a poetry workshop at the New School for Social Research during the spring term. Moved to 791 Broadway, where friends George Montgomery, Dan Wagoner, Donald Droll, and Roy Leaf had lofts. Collaborated with Jasper Johns on poems/lithographs. Traveled to Europe for the opening of the Kline exhibition at Amsterdam's Stedelijk Museum, and for a second showing at Galleria Civica D'Arte Moderna, Turin. Traveled to Antwerp, Paris, Milan, Rome, Copenhagen, Stockholm, Vienna, Zagreb, Belgrade, and Prague. Visited studios of young Dutch artists and met Jan Cremer in Amsterdam. Wrote the subtitles for Alfred Leslie's film *The Last Clean Shirt*, shown at San Francisco Museum of Art and later at Lincoln Center.

1964   *Lunch Poems* published by City Lights Books. Collaborated with Joe Brainard on many collages and drawings. An issue of *Audit/Poetry* published "Featuring Frank O'Hara." *The General Returns from One Place to Another* produced by Present Stages at the Writers Stage Theatre and published in *Art and Literature* in 1965. *Franz Kline: A Retrospective Exhibition* published by Whitechapel Gallery, London. Interviewed David Smith in *David Smith: Sculpting Master of Bolton Landing* and Barnett Newman in *The Continuity of Vision* for the National Educational Television *Art: New York* series.

1965   *Love Poems (Tentative Title)* published by Tibor de Nagy. Curated the *Robert Motherwell* retrospective at the Museum of Modern Art. "Larry Rivers: A Memoir" published in the Larry Rivers retrospective exhibition catalog by Brandeis University. Interviewed by Edward Lucie-Smith for *Studio International*. Helped choose poets invited to Settimano di Poesia, Spoleto Festival of Two Worlds, in the summer. Wrote subtitles for Alfred Leslie's film *Philosophy in the Bedroom*. Featured in the National Educational Television series *USA: Poetry: Frank O'Hara and Ed Sanders*, directed by Richard O. Moore.

1966   Traveled to Europe in the spring to install and introduce the David Smith exhibition in Otterlo, Netherlands. Curated the retrospective and wrote the catalog introduction for the *Nakian* exhibition at the Museum of Modern Art. "Little Elegy for Antonio Machado" published in *Homage to Antonio Machado,* the Tibor de Nagy Gallery exhibition announcement. Died July 25 at Bayview General Hospital, Mastics Beach, Long Island, after being hit and severely injured by a Jeep while he and others stood waiting for the replacement of their disabled beach taxi to take them from Fire Island to Water Island. Buried at the Green River Cemetery in Springs, Long Island. A line from "In Memory of My Feelings," "Grace to be born and live as variously as possible," is carved on his grave stone.

Index of Titles

A NOTE ABOUT THE EDITOR

Mark Ford was born in 1962. He has published several books of poetry and is the author of the critical biography *Raymond Roussel and the Republic of Dreams*. He is a regular contributor to *The New York Review of Books* and *London Review of Books;* he teaches in the English Department at University College London.

A NOTE ON THE TYPE

This book was set in a type called Baskerville. The face itself is a facsimile reproduction of types cast from the molds made for John Baskerville (1706–1775) from his designs. Baskerville's original face was one of the forerunners of the type style known to printers as "modern face"—a "modern" of the period A.D. 1800.

Composed by Creative Graphics,
Allentown, Pennsylvania

Printed and bound by Thomson Shore Inc.,
Dexter, Michigan

Designed by Soonyoung Kwon